New York Yankees 2020

A Baseball Companion

Edited by R.J. Anderson, Craig Goldstein and Bret Sayre

Baseball Prospectus

Craig Brown, Steven Goldman and David Pease, Consultant Editors
Robert Au, Harry Pavlidis and Amy Pircher, Statistics Editors

Library of Congress Cataloging-in-Publication Data:
paperback
ISBN-13: 978-1-949332-82-7

Project Credits
Cover Design: Michael Byzewski at Aesthetic Apparatus
Interior Design and Production: Jeff Pease, Dave Pease
Layout: Jeff Pease, Dave Pease

Baseball icon courtesy of Uberux, from https://www.shareicon.net/author/uberux

Ballpark diagram courtesy of Lou Spirito/THIRTY81 Project, https://thirty81project.com/

Manufactured in the United States of America
10 9 8 7 6 5 4 3 2 1

Table of Contents

Statistical Introduction v

Part 1: Team Analysis

New York Yankees: Where Are You Going, Where Have You Been? 3
Jarrett Seidler, Smith Brickner and Matthew Trueblood

Performance Graphs 7

2019 Team Performance 8

2020 Team Projections 9

Team Personnel 10

Yankee Stadium Stats 11

Yankees Team Analysis 13

Part 2: Player Analysis

Yankees Player Analysis 20

Yankees Prospects 97

Part 3: Featured Articles

The Baseball Is Juiced (Again) 113
Robert Arthur

The Moral Hazard of Playing It Safe 117
Craig Goldstein

Index of Names 123

Statistical Introduction

Sports are, fundamentally, a blend of athletic endeavor and storytelling. Baseball, like any other sport, tells its stories in so many ways: in the arc of a game from the stands or a season from the box scores, in photos, or even in numbers. At Baseball Prospectus, we understand that statistics don't replace observation or any of baseball's stories, but complement everything else that makes the game so much fun.

What stats help us with is with patterns and precision, variance and value. This book can help you learn things you may not see from watching a game or hundred, whether it's the path of a career over time or the breadth of the entire MLB. We'd also never ask you to choose between our numbers and the experience of viewing a game from the cheap seats or the comfort of your home; our publication combines running the numbers with observations and wisdom from some of the brightest minds we can find. But if you *do* want to learn more about the numbers beyond what's on the backs of player jerseys, let us help explain.

Offense

We've revised our methodology for determining batting value. Long-time readers of the book will notice that we've retired True Average in favor of a new metric: Deserved Runs Created Plus (DRC+). Developed by Jonathan Judge and our stats team, this statistic measures everything a player does at the plate–reaching base, hitting for power, making outs, and moving runners over–and puts it on a scale where 100 equals league-average performance. A DRC+ of 150 is terrific, a DRC+ of 100 is average and a DRC+ of 75 means you better be an excellent defender.

DRC+ also does a better job than any of our previous metrics in taking contextual factors into account. The model adjusts for how the park affects performance, but also for things like the talent of the opposing pitcher, value of different types of batted-ball events, league, temperature and other factors. It's able to describe a player's expected offensive contribution than any other statistic we've found over the years, and also does a better job of predicting future performance as well.

There's a lot more to DRC+'s story, and you can read all about it in greater depth near the end of this book.

The other aspect of run-scoring is baserunning, which we quantify using Baserunning Runs. BRR not only records the value of stolen bases (or getting caught in the act), but also accounts for all the stuff that doesn't show up on the back of a baseball card: a runner's ability to go first to third on a single, or advance on a fly ball.

Defense

Where offensive value is *relatively* easy to identify and understand, defensive value is...not. Over the past dozen years, the sabermetric community has focused mostly on stats based on zone data: a real-live human person records the type of batted ball and estimated landing location, and models are created that give expected outs. From there, you can compare fielders' actual outs to those expected ones. Simple, right?

Unfortunately, zone data has two major issues. First, zone data is recorded by commercial data providers who keep the raw data private unless you pay for it. (All the statistics we build in this book and on our website use public data as inputs.) That hurts our ability to test assumptions or duplicate results. Second, over the years it has become apparent that there's quite a bit of "noise" in zone-based fielding analysis. Sometimes the conclusions drawn from zone data don't hold up to scrutiny, and sometimes the different data provided by different providers don't look anything alike, giving wildly different results. Sometimes the hard-working professional stringers or scorers might unknowingly inflict unconscious bias into the mix: for example good fielders will often be credited with more expected outs despite the data, and ballparks with high press boxes tend to score more line drives than ones with a lower press box.

Enter our Fielding Runs Above Average (FRAA). For most positions, FRAA is built from play-by-play data, which allows us to avoid the subjectivity found in many other fielding metrics. The idea is this: count how many fielding plays are made by a given player and compare that to expected plays for an average fielder at their position (based on pitcher ground ball tendencies and batter handedness). Then we adjust for park and base-out situations.

When it comes to catchers, our methodology is a little different thanks to the laundry list of responsibilities they're tasked with beyond just, well, catching and throwing the ball. By now you've probably heard about "framing" or the art of making umpires more likely to call balls outside the strike zone for strikes. To put this into one tidy number, we incorporate pitch tracking data (for the years it exists) and adjust for important factors like pitcher, umpire, batter and home-field advantage using a mixed-model approach. This grants us a number for how many strikes the catcher is personally adding to (or subtracting from) his pitchers' performance...which we then convert to runs added or lost using linear weights.

Framing is one of the biggest parts of determining catcher value, but we also take into account blocking balls from going past, whether a scorer deems it a passed ball or a wild pitch. We use a similar approach—one that really benefits from the pitch tracking data that tells us what ends up in the dirt and what doesn't. We also include a catcher's ability to prevent stolen bases and how well they field balls in play, and *finally* we come up with our FRAA for catchers.

Pitching

Both pitching and fielding make up the half of baseball that isn't run scoring: run prevention. Separating pitching from fielding is a tough task, and most recent pitching analysis has branched off from Voros McCracken's famous (and controversial) statement, "There is little if any difference among major-league pitchers in their ability to prevent hits on balls hit in the field of play." The research of the analytic community has validated this to some extent, and there are a host of "defense-independent" pitching measures that have been developed to try and extract the effect of the defense behind a hurler from the pitcher's work.

Our solution to this quandary is Deserved Run Average (DRA), our core pitching metric. DRA looks like earned run average (ERA), the tried-and-true pitching stat you've seen on every baseball broadcast or box score from the past century, but it's very different. To start, DRA takes an event-by-event look at what the pitchers does, and adjusts the value of that event based on different environmental factors like park, batter, catcher, umpire, base-out situation, run differential, inning, defense, home field advantage, pitcher role and temperature. That mixed model gives us a pitcher's expected contribution, similar to what we do for our DRC+ model for hitters and FRAA model for catchers. (Oh, and we also consider the pitcher's effect on basestealing and on balls getting past the catcher.)

It's important to note that DRA is set to the scale of runs allowed per nine innings (RA9) instead of ERA, which makes DRA's scale slightly higher than ERA's. The reason for this is because ERA tends to overrate three types of pitchers:

1. Pitchers who play in parks where scorers hand out more errors. Official scorers differ significantly in the frequency at which they assign errors to fielders.
2. Ground-ball pitchers, because a substantial proportion of errors occur on groundballs.
3. Pitchers who aren't very good. Better pitchers often allow fewer unearned runs than bad pitchers, because good pitchers tend to find ways to get out of jams.

Since the last time you picked up an edition of this book, we've also made a few minor changes to DRA to make it better. Recent research into "tunneling"—the act of throwing consecutive pitches that appear similar from a batter's point of view until after the swing decision point–data has given us a new contextual factor to account for in DRA: plate distance. This refers to the distance between successive pitches as they approach the plate, and while it has a smaller effect than factors like velocity or whiff rate, it still can help explain pitcher strikeout rate in our model.

New Pitching Metrics for 2020

We're including a few "new" pitching metrics in the book for the 2020 edition, though unlike last year, these numbers may be a little bit more familiar to those of you who have spent some time investigating baseball statistics.

Fastball Percentage

Our fastball percentage (FB%) statistic measures how frequently a pitcher throws a pitch classified as a "fastball," measured as a percentage of overall pitches thrown. We qualify three types of fastballs:

1. The traditional four-seam fastball;
2. The two-seam fastball or sinker;
3. "Hard cutters," which are pitches that have the movement profile of a cut fastball and are used as the pitcher's primary offering or in place of a more traditional fastball.

For example, a pitcher with a FB% of 67 throws any combination of these three pitches about two-thirds of the time.

Whiff Rate

Everybody loves a swing and a miss, and whiff rate (WHF) measures how frequently pitchers induce a swinging strike. To calculate WHF, we add up all the pitches thrown that ended with a swinging strike, then divide that number by a pitcher's total pitches thrown. Most often, high whiff rates correlate with high strikeout rates (and overall effective pitcher performance).

Called Strike Probability

Called Strike Probability (CSP) is a number that represents the likelihood that all of a pitcher's pitches will be called a strike while controlling for location, pitcher and batter handedness, umpire and count. Here's how it works: on each pitch, our model determines how many times (out of 100) that a similar pitch was called for a strike given those factors mentioned above, and when normalized for each batter's strike zone. Then we average the CSP for all pitches thrown by a pitcher in a season, and that gives us the yearly CSP percentage you see in the stats boxes.

As you might imagine, pitchers with a higher CSP are more likely to work in the zone, where pitchers with a lower CSP are likely locating their pitches outside the normal strike zone, for better or for worse.

Projections

Many of you aren't turning to this book just for a look at what a player has done, but for a look at what a player is going to do: the PECOTA projections. PECOTA, initially developed by Nate Silver (who has moved on to greater fame as a political analyst), consists of three parts:

1. Major-league equivalencies, which use minor-league statistics to project how a player will perform in the major leagues;
2. Baseline forecasts, which use weighted averages and regression to the mean to estimate a player's current true talent level; and
3. Aging curves, which uses the career paths of comparable players to estimate how a player's statistics are likely to change over time.

With all those important things covered, let's take a look at what's in the book this year.

Team Prospectus

Most of this book is composed of team chapters, with one for each of the 30 major-league franchises. On the first page of each chapter, you'll see a box that contains some of the key statistics for each team as well as a very inviting stadium diagram. (You can see an example of this for the Milwaukee Brewers on this very page!)

We start with the team name, their unadjusted 2019 win-loss record, and their divisional ranking. Beneath that are a host of other team statistics. **Pythag** presents an adjusted 2019 winning percentage, calculated by taking runs scored per game (**RS/G**) and runs allowed per game (**RA/G**) for the team, and running them through a version of Bill James' Pythagorean formula that was refined and improved by David Smyth and Brandon Heipp. (The formula is called "Pythagenpat," which is equally fun to type and to say.)

Next up is **DRC+**, described earlier, to indicate the overall hitting ability of the team either above or below league-average. Run prevention on the pitching side is covered by **DRA** (also mentioned earlier) and another metric: Fielding Independent Pitching (**FIP**), which calculates another ERA-like statistic based on strikeouts, walks, and home runs recorded. Defensive Efficiency Rating (**DER**) tells us the percentage of balls in play turned into outs for the team, and is a quick fielding shorthand that rounds out run prevention.

After that, we have several measures related to roster composition, as opposed to on-field performance. **B-Age** and **P-Age** tell us the average age of a team's batters and pitchers, respectively. **Salary** is the combined team payroll for all on-field players, and Doug Pappas' Marginal Dollars per Marginal Win (**M$/MW**) tells us how much money a team spent to earn production above replacement level.

Ending this batch of statistics is the number of disabled list days a team had over the season (**IL Days**) and the amount of salary paid to players on the disabled list (**$ on IL**); this final number is expressed as a percentage of total payroll.

Next to each of these stats, we've listed each team's MLB rank in that category from first to 30th. In this, first always indicates a positive outcome and 30th a negative outcome, except in the case of salary—first is highest.

After the franchise statistics, we share a few items about the team's home ballpark. There's the aforementioned diagram of the park's dimensions (including distances to the outfield wall), a graphic showing the height of the wall from the left-field pole to the right-field pole, and a table showing three-year park factors for the stadium. The park factors are displayed as indexes where 100 is average, 110 means that the park inflates the statistic in question by 10 percent, and 90 means that the park deflates the statistic in question by 10 percent.

On the second page of each team chapter, you'll find three graphs. The first is the **2019 Hit List Ranking**. This shows our Hit List Rank for the team on each day of the 2019 season and is intended to give you a picture of the ups and downs of the team's season. Hit List Rank measures overall team performance and drives the Hit List Power Rankings at the baseballprospectus.com website.

The second graph is **Committed Payroll** and helps you see how the team's payroll has compared to the MLB and divisional average payrolls over time. Payroll figures are current as of January 1, 2020; with so many free agents still unsigned as of this writing, the final 2020 figure will likely be significantly different for many teams. (In the meantime, you can always find the most current data at Baseball Prospectus' Cot's Baseball Contracts page.)

The third graph is **Farm System Ranking** and displays how the Baseball Prospectus prospect team has ranked the organization's farm system since 2007.

After the graphs, we have a **Personnel** section that lists many of the important decision-makers and upper-level field and operations staff members for the franchise, as well as any former Baseball Prospectus staff members who are currently part of the organization. (In very rare circumstances, someone might be on both lists!)

Juan Soto LF

Born: 10/25/98 Age: 21 Bats: L Throws: L
Height: 6'1" Weight: 185 Origin: International Free Agent, 2015

YEAR	TEAM	LVL	AGE	PA	R	2B	3B	HR	RBI	BB	K	SB	CS	AVG/OBP/SLG
2017	NAT	RK	18	27	3	1	1	0	4	2	1	0	0	.320/.370/.440
2017	HAG	A	18	96	15	5	0	3	14	10	8	1	2	.360/.427/.523
2018	HAG	A	19	74	12	5	3	5	24	14	13	2	0	.373/.486/.814
2018	POT	A+	19	73	17	3	1	7	18	11	8	0	1	.371/.466/.790
2018	HAR	AA	19	35	4	2	0	2	10	4	7	1	0	.323/.400/.581
2018	WAS	MLB	19	494	77	25	1	22	70	79	99	5	2	.292/.406/.517
2019	WAS	MLB	20	659	110	32	5	34	110	108	132	12	1	.282/.401/.548
2020	*WAS*	*MLB*	*21*	*630*	*92*	*30*	*3*	*35*	*102*	*85*	*123*	*5*	*2*	*.284/.382/.543*

Comparables: Ronald Acuña Jr., Mike Trout, Tony Conigliaro

YEAR	TEAM	LVL	AGE	PA	DRC+	VORP	BABIP	BRR	FRAA	WARP
2017	NAT	RK	18	27	135	1.5	.333	0.0	RF(9): -1.1	0.0
2017	HAG	A	18	96	181	8.0	.373	1.0	RF(19): -1.9, LF(2): -0.3	0.9
2018	HAG	A	19	74	222	14.5	.405	0.3	RF(14): 1.1, CF(2): 0.2	1.2
2018	POT	A+	19	73	260	15.4	.340	1.4	RF(14): 1.0, LF(1): 0.0	1.6
2018	HAR	AA	19	35	113	3.6	.364	0.0	LF(4): 0.6, RF(4): -0.5	0.1
2018	WAS	MLB	19	494	125	40.5	.338	-0.5	LF(114): 2.7	3.0
2019	WAS	MLB	20	659	136	49.0	.312	1.4	LF(150): -0.8	4.9
2020	*WAS*	*MLB*	*21*	*630*	*133*	*43.6*	*.310*	*-0.1*	*LF 3*	*4.8*

Position Players

After all that information and a thoughtful bylined essay covering each team, we present our player comments. These are also bylined, but due to frequent franchise shifts during the offseason, our bylines are more a rough guide than a perfect accounting of who wrote what.

Each player is listed with the major-league team that employed him as of early January 2020. If a player changed teams after that point via free agency, trade, or any other method, you'll be able to find them in the chapter for their previous squad.

As an example, take a look at the player comment for Nationals outfielder Juan Soto: the stat block that accompanies his written comment is at the top of this page. First we cover biographical information (age is as of June 30, 2020) before moving onto the stats themselves. Our statistic columns include standard identifying information like **YEAR**, **TEAM**, **LVL** (level of affiliated play) and **AGE** before getting into the numbers. Next, we provide raw, untranslated numbers like you might find on the back of your dad's baseball cards: **PA** (plate appearances), **R** (runs), **2B** (doubles), **3B** (triples), **HR** (home runs), **RBI** (runs batted in), **BB** (walks), **K** (strikeouts), **SB** (stolen bases) and **CS** (caught stealing).

Next, we have unadjusted "slash" statistics: **AVG** (batting average), **OBP** (on-base percentage) and **SLG** (slugging percentage). Following the slash line is **DRC+** (Deserved Runs Created Plus), which we described earlier as total offensive expected contribution compared to the league average.

One of our oldest active metrics, **VORP** (Value Over Replacement Player), considers offensive production, position and plate appearances. In essence, it is the number of runs contributed beyond what a replacement-level player at the same position would contribute if given the same percentage of team plate appearances. VORP does not consider the quality of a player's defense.

BABIP (batting average on balls in play) tells us how often a ball in play fell for a hit, and can help us identify whether a batter may have been lucky or not...but note that high BABIPs also tend to follow the great hitters of our time, as well as speedy singles hitters who put the ball on the ground.

The next item is **BRR** (Baserunning Runs), which covers all of a player's baserunning accomplishments including (but not limited to) swiped bags and failed attempts. Next is **FRAA** (Fielding Runs Above Average), which also includes the number of games previously played at each position noted in parentheses. Multi-position players have only their two most frequent positions listed here, but their total FRAA number reflects all positions played.

Our last column here is **WARP** (Wins Above Replacement Player). WARP estimates the total value of a player, which means for hitters it takes into account hitting runs above average (calculated using the DRC+ model), BRR and FRAA. Then, it makes an adjustment for positions played and gives the player a credit for plate appearances based upon the difference between "replacement level"—which is derived from the quality of players added to a team's roster after the start of the season–and the league average.

The final line just below the stats box is **PECOTA** data, which is discussed further in a following section.

Catchers

Catchers are a special breed, and thus they have earned their own separate box which displays some of the defensive metrics that we've built just for them. As an example, let's check out J.T. Realmuto.

The **YEAR** and **TEAM** columns match what you'd find in the other stat box. **P. COUNT** indicates the number of pitches thrown while the catcher was behind the plate, including swinging strikes, fouls and balls in play. **FRM RUNS** is the total run value the catcher provided (or cost) his team by influencing the umpire to call strikes where other catchers did not. **BLK RUNS** expresses the total run value above or below average for the catcher's ability to prevent wild pitches and passed balls. **THRW RUNS** is calculated using a similar model as the previous two statistics, and it measures a catcher's ability to throw out basestealers but also to dissuade them from testing his arm in the first place. It takes into account factors like the pitcher (including his delivery and pickoff move) and baserunner (who could be as fast as Billy Hamilton or as slow as Yonder Alonso). **TOT RUNS** is the sum of all of the previous three statistics.

Justin Verlander RHP

Born: 02/20/83 Age: 37 Bats: R Throws: R
Height: 6'5" Weight: 225 Origin: Round 1, 2004 Draft (#2 overall)

YEAR	TEAM	LVL	AGE	W	L	SV	G	GS	IP	H	HR	BB/9	K/9	K	GB%	BABIP
2017	DET	MLB	34	10	8	0	28	28	172	153	23	3.5	9.2	176	34%	.283
2017	HOU	MLB	34	5	0	0	5	5	34	17	4	1.3	11.4	43	32%	.194
2018	HOU	MLB	35	16	9	0	34	34	214	156	28	1.6	12.2	290	31%	.272
2019	HOU	MLB	36	21	6	0	34	34	223	137	36	1.7	12.1	300	36%	.219
2020	*HOU*	*MLB*	*37*	*15*	*6*	*0*	*29*	*29*	*184*	*138*	*28*	*2.3*	*12.1*	*248*	*35%*	*.274*

Comparables: Zack Greinke, A.J. Burnett, Aníbal Sánchez

YEAR	TEAM	LVL	AGE	WHIP	ERA	DRA	WARP	MPH	FB%	WHF	CSP
2017	DET	MLB	34	1.28	3.82	4.03	3.0	97.7	58	11	47.8
2017	HOU	MLB	34	0.65	1.06	3.08	0.9	97.5	59.6	15.1	49.9
2018	HOU	MLB	35	0.90	2.52	2.33	7.3	97.5	61.2	16.2	51.6
2019	HOU	MLB	36	0.80	2.58	2.51	7.9	96.8	49.9	17.5	48.3
2020	*HOU*	*MLB*	*37*	*1.01*	*2.75*	*2.95*	*5.3*	*95.8*	*54.6*	*15.1*	*48.2*

Pitchers

Let's give our pitchers a turn, using 2019 AL Cy Young winner Justin Verlander as our example. Take a look at his stat block: the first line and the **YEAR, TEAM, LVL** and **AGE** columns are the same as in the position player example earlier.

Here too, we have a series of columns that display raw, unadjusted statistics compiled by the pitcher over the course of a season: **W** (wins), **L** (losses), **SV** (saves), **G** (games pitched), **GS** (games started), **IP** (innings pitched), **H** (hits allowed) and **HR** (home runs allowed). Next we have two statistics that are rates: **BB/9** (walks per nine innings) and **K/9** (strikeouts per nine innings), before returning to the unadjusted K (strikeouts).

Next up is **GB%** (ground ball percentage), which is the percentage of all batted balls that were hit on the ground, including both outs and hits. Remember, this is based on observational data and subject to human error, so please approach this with a healthy dose of skepticism.

BABIP (batting average on balls in play) is calculated using the same methodology as it is for position players, but it often tells us more about a pitcher than it does a hitter. With pitchers, a high BABIP is often due to poor defense or bad luck, and can often be an indicator of potential rebound, and a low BABIP may be cause to expect performance regression. (A typical league-average BABIP is close to .290-.300.)

The metrics **WHIP** (walks plus hits per inning pitched) and **ERA** (earned run average) are old standbys: WHIP measures walks and hits allowed on a per-inning basis, while ERA measures earned runs on a nine-inning basis. Neither of these stats are translated or adjusted.

DRA (Deserved Run Average) was described at length earlier, and measures how many runs the pitcher "deserved" to allow per nine innings. Please note that since we lack all the data points that would make for a "real" DRA for minor-league events, the DRA displayed for minor league partial-seasons is based off of different data. (That data is a modified version of our cFIP metric, which you can find more information about on our website.)

Just like with hitters, **WARP** (Wins Above Replacement Player) is a total value metric that puts pitchers of all stripes on the same scale as position players. We use DRA as the primary input for our calculation of WARP. You might notice that relief pitchers (due to their limited innings) may have a lower WARP than you were expecting or than you might see in other WARP-like metrics. WARP does not take leverage into account, just the actions a pitcher performs and the expected value of those actions...which ends up judging high-leverage relief pitchers differently than you might imagine given their prestige and market value.

MPH gives you the pitcher's 95th percentile velocity for the noted season, in order to give you an idea of what the *peak* fastball velocity a pitcher possesses. Since this comes from our pitch-tracking data, it is not publicly available for minor-league pitchers.

Finally, we display the three new pitching metrics we described earlier. **FB%** (fastball percentage) gives you the percentage of fastballs thrown out of all pitches. **WHF** (whiff rate) tells you the percentage of swinging strikes induced out of all pitches. **CSP** (called strike probability) expresses the likelihood of all pitches thrown to result in a called strike, after controlling for factors like handedness, umpire, pitch type, count and location.

PECOTA

All players have PECOTA projections for 2020, as well as a set of other numbers that describe the performance of comparable players according to PECOTA. All projections for 2020 are for the player at the date we went to press in early January and are projected into the league and park context as indicated by the team abbreviation. (Note that players at very low levels of the minors are too unpredictable to assess using these numbers.) All PECOTA projected statistics represent a player's projected major-league performance.

Below the projections are the player's three highest-scoring comparable players as determined by PECOTA. All comparables represent a snapshot of how the listed player was performing at the same age as the current player, so if a

23-year-old pitcher is compared to Bartolo Colón, he's actually being compared to a 23-year-old Colón, not the version that pitched for the Rangers in 2018, nor to Colón's career as a whole.

A few points about pitcher projections. First, we aren't yet projecting peak velocity, so that column will be blank in the PECOTA lines. Second, projecting DRA is trickier than evaluating past performance, because it is unclear how deserving each pitcher will be of his anticipated outcomes. However, we know that another DRA-related statistic–contextual FIP or cFIP-estimates future run scoring very well. So for PECOTA, the projected DRA figures you see are based on the past cFIPs generated by the pitcher and comparable players over time, along with the other factors described above.

Lineouts

In each chapter's Lineouts section, you'll find abbreviated text comments, as well as all the same information you'd find in our full player comments. The only difference is that we limit the stats boxes in this section to only including the 2019 information for each player.

Managers

After all those wonderful team chapters, we've got statistics for each big-league manager, all of whom are organized by alphabetical order. Here you'll find a block including an extraordinary amount of information collected from each manager's entire career. For more information on the acronyms and what they mean, please visit the Glossary at www.baseballprospectus.com.

There is one important metric that we'd like to call attention to, and you'll find it next to each manager's name: **wRM+** (weighted reliever management plus). Developed by Rob Arthur and Rian Watt, wRM+ investigates how good a manager is at using their best relievers during the moments of highest leverage, using both our proprietary DRA metric as well as Leverage Index. wRM+ is scaled to a league average of 100, and a wRM+ of 105 indicates that relievers were used approximately five percent "better" than average. On the other hand, a wRM+ of 95 would tell us the team used its relievers five percent "worse" than the average team.

While wRM+ does not have an extremely strong correlation with a manager, it is statistically significant; this means that a manager is not *entirely* responsible for a team's wRM+, but does have some effect on that number.

PECOTA Leaderboards

If you're familiar with PECOTA, then you'll have noticed that the projection system often appears bullish on players coming off a bad year and bearish on players coming off a good year. (This is because the system weights several previous seasons, not just the most recent one.) In addition, we publish the 50th percentile projections for each player–which is smack in the middle of the range of projected production—which tends to mean PECOTA stat lines don't often have extreme results like 40 home runs or 250 strikeouts in a given season. In essence, PECOTA doesn't project very many extreme seasons.

At the end of the book, we've ranked the top players at each position based on their PECOTA projections. This might help you visualize just how a given player's projection compares to that of their peers, so that even if a dramatic stat line isn't projected, you can still imagine how they stack up against the rest of the league. ■

Part 1: Team Analysis

New York Yankees: Where Are You Going, Where Have You Been?

Jarrett Seidler, Smith Brickner and Matthew Trueblood

2019: What Went Right

It's a good season when you push the best team in your league to Game 6 of the LCS and nearly force a Game 7. The Yankees won 103 games, third-most in baseball, and had the AL East more or less wrapped up by the trade deadline. That is a good season, right?

The thing that went the most right was a modestly controversial offseason signing. The Yankees signed longtime Rockies second baseman DJ LeMahieu—a superlative defender who had only hit at Coors Field—to a two-year, $24 million contract in January. They didn't have second base open with rising superstar Gleyber Torres planted there (or planted there once Didi Gregorius made a successful return from Tommy John surgery the previous October), but they decided to use LeMahieu around the infield. It was Schrodinger's contract; if you believed in his DRC+ and FRAA showing him as a significant contributor on both sides of the ball you thought it was a steal, but if you believed his value was wrapped up in second base defense and Coors-aided offense you thought it was a disaster.

The ayes had it: LeMahieu defied all expectations and showed more like a $240 million player. He hit .327/.375/.518, threatened to win his second batting title, set career highs in DRC+ and home runs despite moving away from Coors, and played at least 40 games at second, third, and first. It was the best season of his career, and it earned him a fourth-place finish in the MVP balloting.

Joining him as an infield sensation was Gio Urshela. The Yankees picked up the journeyman third baseman from the Blue Jays late in the 2018 season and stashed him in Triple-A until a week into the 2019 season. When the Yankees were pressed into calling him up he shocked the league with an All-Star caliber season.

Urshela has always been a stellar defender at the hot corner, and years and years ago it seemed like he had offensive promise too; it just took him until he was 27 to figure it out.

Mike Tauchman had a similar story to Urshela's but in the outfield. Cameron Maybin came along in an in-season minor league trade and contributed, too. The Yankees got very strong play from guys who weren't even on the radar to start the season. Many of the stars continued to shine as well, with a strong renaissance from Brett Gardner and continued emergence from budding superstar Torres.

What Went Wrong

They didn't win the World Series. The Yankees define themselves not by contention, but by rings. The 2010s were the first decade since the 1980s where they didn't win the World Series, and the first decade since the 1910s in which they didn't win an American League pennant. For any other franchise, 2019 would've been a successful capstone to a 10-year run of sustained contention. For this franchise, it's almost a failure.

The Yankees generally got pretty good performances when they could keep their players on the field, but they had quite a time doing so. Gregorius was expected to miss the beginning of the season with Tommy John surgery, and along with the long-since forgotten Troy Tulowitzki, LeMahieu was in part expected to cover that vacancy with Torres sliding to short. That part went somewhat as planned, at least, although Gregorius didn't hit much after coming back.

Unfortunately, by the time he did return, other vacancies had opened. It started when third baseman Miguel Andújar tore his labrum in March. He made a valiant effort at rehabilitation but got in only a handful of games before having season-ending surgery. Right behind him was first baseman Greg Bird, who had a season-ending foot injury in April. That combination opened the door for Urshela's huge breakout season. Luke Voit battled abdominal and groin problems for most of the second half of the season.

Star slugger Giancarlo Stanton only played in 18 games. It wasn't even one long injury for Stanton. He played a season-long game of Operation, missing time in the regular season with biceps, shoulder, calf, and knee problems, and then pulled his quad in the playoffs. Fellow outfielder Aaron Hicks missed the majority of the season with back and elbow problems. Aaron Judge played more than Hicks but missed significant time with a strained oblique. The Yankees survived due to the aforementioned unexpectedly strong contributions elsewhere, but it wasn't ideal.

And yet there was still more: Luis Severino was supposed to anchor the rotation; he missed the first five months with shoulder woes. Dellin Betances was supposed to anchor the bullpen; he also didn't show up until September with shoulder woes, then tore his Achilles in his first outing. We're not even going into any of the smaller injuries, because you probably get the point by now. *—Jarrett Seidler*

Prospect Outlook

The Yankees system has lost some of its luster because of trades and recent prospect graduations, but that's not to say there isn't talent here. Right-handed pitcher **Deivi García** had a breakout campaign in which he became a Top 50 prospect and surged to Triple-A at age 20. Besides Garcia, however, much of the organization's talent resides in the low minors.

At the forefront of this low minors movement is **Jasson Dominguez**, the prized outfield prospect who the team used nearly all of its 2019 international bonus pool to sign. Tabbed as "The Martian" for his otherworldly abilities, Dominguez's professional experience is limited to Tricky League ball, but he is a must-watch and could be a fast riser if initial reports are accurate. Otherwise, a majority of the excitement stems around their collection of power arms. **Luis Medina**, **Luis Gil**, **Yoendrys Gomez**, and **Roansy Contreras** have all had varying degrees of positive reports. Positional prospects such as **Estevan Florial**, **Ezequiel Duran** and **Anthony Volpe** are also cause for excitement, though the latter two are several years away from contributing and Florial struggled with injuries for a second consecutive year. *—Smith Brickner*

2020 Outlook

In one sense, it makes sense that if you commit $324 million to a single player, that pretty much leaves you set for the balance of the winter. In the Yankees' case, however, it feels profoundly odd. Gerrit Cole is a transformative signing for them; he stabilizes the rotation and gives it the elite upside it had been missing. However, Brian Cashman's front office more or less stopped there. Austin Romine departed as a free agent, and the team replaced him only by signing a trio of veterans to minor-league deals. Kyle Higashioka is the presumptive backup to Gary Sánchez, who isn't exactly a bastion of health or consistency. Aaron Hicks will surely miss some portion of 2020, having had Tommy John surgery in late October, but the team only felt the need to bring in glove-first fringe guys on minor-league deals there, too.

The team did re-sign Gardner, and most of their other key contributors will return. Still, the roster has a slightly incomplete feeling. The team is very high on the change they made in athletic training and injury prevention, which would obviously be a change as significant as the addition of Cole, but they're investing a lot of their trust in that particular change, despite an aging roster and some players with obvious deficiencies even when healthy. *—Matthew Trueblood*

Performance Graphs

2019 Hit List Ranking

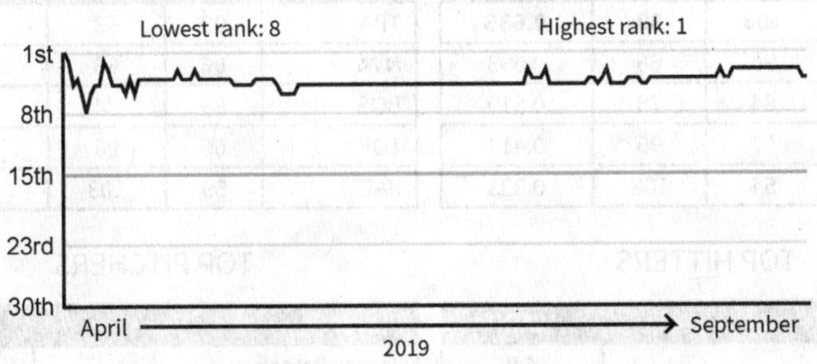

Committed Payroll (in millions)

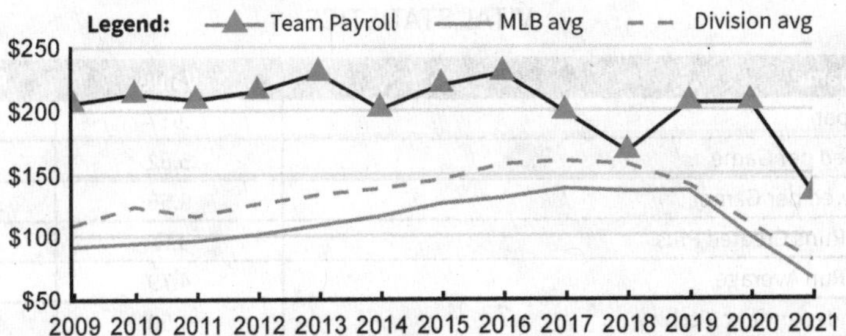

Farm System Ranking

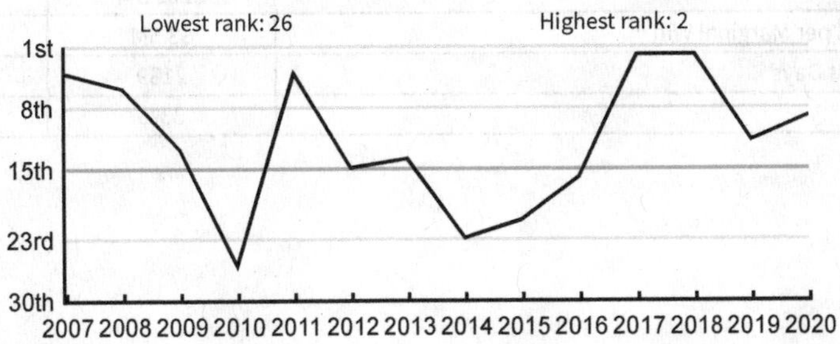

2019 Team Performance

ACTUAL STANDINGS

Team	W	L	Pct
NYA	**103**	**59**	**0.636**
TBA	96	66	0.593
BOS	84	78	0.519
TOR	67	95	0.414
BAL	54	108	0.333

THIRD-ORDER STANDINGS

Team	W	L	Pct
TBA	99	63	0.613
NYA	**96**	**66**	**0.590**
BOS	88	74	0.544
TOR	66	96	0.410
BAL	59	103	0.363

TOP HITTERS

Player	WARP
DJ LeMahieu	4.8
Gleyber Torres	3.9
Aaron Judge	3.6

TOP PITCHERS

Player	WARP
James Paxton	2.6
Domingo Germán	2.3
Tommy Kahnle	2.0

VITAL STATISTICS

Statistic Name	Value	Rank
Pythagenpat	.617	3rd
Runs Scored per Game	5.82	1st
Runs Allowed per Game	4.56	11th
Deserved Runs Created Plus	112	3rd
Deserved Run Average	4.79	13th
Fielding Independent Pitching	4.50	17th
Defensive Efficiency Rating	.703	16th
Batter Age	28.3	21st
Pitcher Age	30.0	26th
Salary	$203.9M	3rd
Marginal $ per Marginal Win	$3.5M	19th
Injured List Days	2189	30th
$ on IL	33%	29th

2020 Team Projections

PROJECTED STANDINGS

Team	W	L	Pct	+/-
NYA	**99.0**	**63.0**	**0.611**	**-4**
TBA	87.3	74.7	0.539	-9
BOS	84.5	77.5	0.522	0
TOR	76.6	85.4	0.473	10
BAL	62.9	99.1	0.388	9

TOP PROJECTED HITTERS

Player	WARP
DJ LeMahieu	5.3
Aaron Judge	3.8
Giancarlo Stanton	3.4

TOP PROJECTED PITCHERS

Player	WARP
Gerrit Cole	5.3
Luis Severino	2.4
James Paxton	1.8

FARM SYSTEM REPORT

Top Prospect	Number of Top 101 Prospects
Deivi Garcia, #24	2

KEY DEDUCTIONS

Player	WARP
Edwin Encarnación	1.9
Didi Gregorius	1.6
Dellin Betances	1.6
Cameron Maybin	0.9
Austin Romine	0.3
Greg Bird	0.0
Stephen Tarpley	0.0
Cory Gearrin	-0.1
Nestor Cortes Jr.	-0.2

KEY ADDITIONS

Player	WARP
Gerrit Cole	5.3
Domingo Germán	0.7
Deivi Garcia	0.3
Brooks Kriske	0.1
Miguel Yajure	0.1
Luis Gil	0.1
Estevan Florial	0.0
Erik Kratz	0.0
Nick Nelson	0.0
Luis Medina	-0.1

Team Personnel

Senior Vice President, General Manager
Brian Cashman

Senior Vice President, Assistant General Manager
Jean Afterman, Esq.

Vice President, Assistant General Manager
Michael Fishman

Vice President, Baseball Operations
Tim Naehring

Manager
Aaron Boone

Yankee Stadium Stats

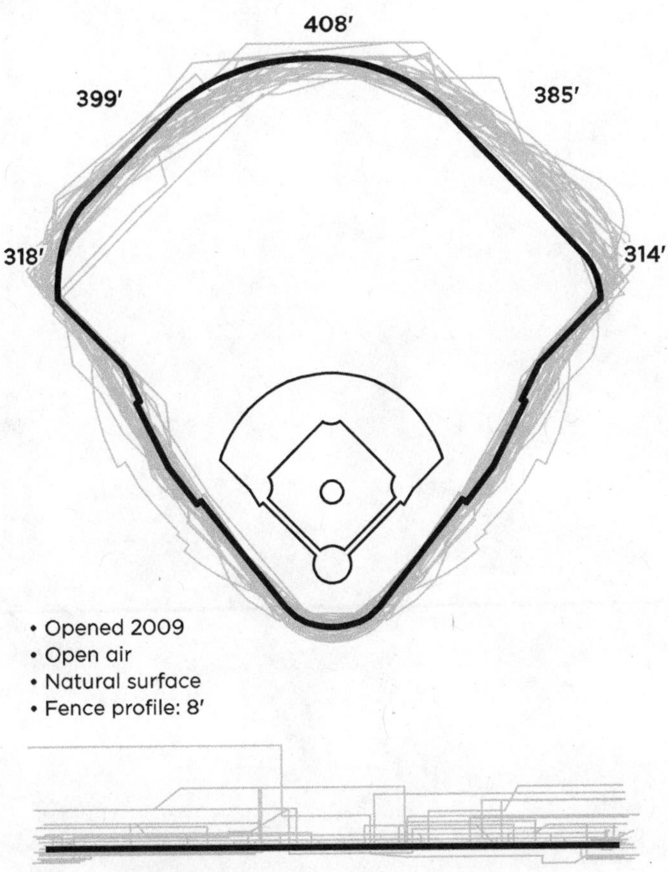

- Opened 2009
- Open air
- Natural surface
- Fence profile: 8′

Three-Year Park Factors

Runs	Runs/RH	Runs/LH	HR/RH	HR/LH
100	101	100	104	111

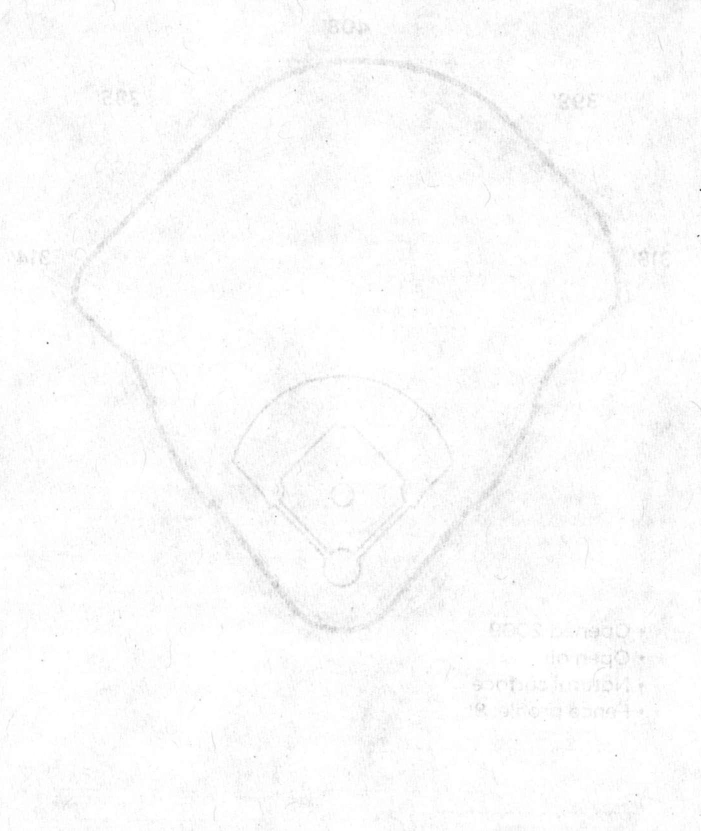

Yankees Team Analysis

Right as the playoffs began, Major League Baseball lugged its skateboard behind its back, turned its bent brim cap backward, snuck into the local middle school with its finest unlicensed band tee and unveiled a string of snappy hashtags for the postseason—surely enough to draw fellow kids to America's Pastime.

#WePlayLoud was one slogan, mixing in black and white footage of baseball games with young stars like Alex Bregman pimping out home-run trots. (Bregman would apologize for staring down a World Series Game 6 home run.) The others were team-specific hashtags of varying quality. As a baseball fan who, though no longer all that young has attempted to remain youthful—I use moisturizer and occasionally clean my sneakers (try it, dads)—I had opinions on how well the hashtagged slogans seized the essence of the team and its supporters.

Some captured its fanbase but failed to endear them to young people, or, Lord willing, anyone else. For example, the Braves' #ChopOn rendered the essence of fans who pack their Cobb County stadium to perform demeaning caricature in unison. But, as the organization learned when Cherokee Nation citizen and Cardinals reliever Ryan Helsley expressed his frustrations, their atonal and tone-deaf gesture just don't slap as hard when sharing the field with the object of your mimicry.

Other slogans deserve as much scrutiny as effort put into them by the league. Even if Toby Hall, Jorge Cantu and Dewon Brazelton jointly requested a 2,000-word essay on the meaning of #RaysUp, sorry to say, I could not oblige.

Then there's the Yankees' #NextManUp. It's not an artful turn of phrase, but it sure as hell represented the Yankees, who succeeded by cycling through retreads and late bloomers, even if forging a deep team came at the expense of fielding a complete one.

The Yankees came into 2019 with a 100-win Wild Card team and more than a few superstars like Aaron Judge, 2017 NL MVP Giancarlo Stanton and Luis Severino, each comfortably recognized among the inner circle of the best players alive. All of them spent time on the shelf.

Severino and Aaron Hicks, both recipients of owner-friendly extensions before the season began, lost significant time to injuries suffered in spring training. Severino and relief ace Dellin Betances, in particular, were in injury sync, battling shoulder and lat issues that almost wiped out their entire year. Stanton led the team in games played the year prior, his first in New York, but managed just 72 plate appearances in 2019. So, injuries bested the staff ace, relief ace, heart-of-the-order-slugger, starting shortstop and $70-million dollar center fielder—that's enough significant injuries for one year right? Heh.

Miguel Andújar, who was a Rookie of the Year Award runner-up in 2018, needed season-ending shoulder surgery. Greg Bird has more or less made his nest on the injured list since 2016. Luke Voit, acquired in a minor (at the time) deal for Giovanny Gallegos, was detected by their analytics department and did nothing but hit as the primary first baseman in 2018. He was going almost as strong until a sports hernia derailed his second half. This is but a taste of the 2019 Yankees' injury problems—they sent a record 30 players to the IL over the course of the season, resulting in 600 more days lost to injury than any other team, per Spotrac. So, why didn't they suck? All those #NextManUps, of course.

DJ LeMahieu was acquired as a high-usage utility player, but the 30-year-old became one of the Yankees' primary infielders, and then their first baseman throughout the playoffs. He was the first and greatest #NextManUp. LeMahieu alone couldn't run away with the division, not with all the injuries.

Gio Urshela was DFA'd by the Blue Jays last summer, and pressed into duty with Andújar's injury. He responded with outstanding work on both sides of the ball, challenging for the batting title late into the season while slugging .539 (his career OPS was .589 before he donned pinstripes).

There was Cameron Maybin, once a super prospect traded for Miguel Cabrera, who was a journeyman cut by the Giants before the season began and traded to the Yankees after hitting .229/.397/.292 for Triple-A Columbus. Marcus Thames told Maybin to "use his good swing," and "hit the ball hard." Sounds too simple, but the 32-year-old added four degrees to his launch angle and slugged a career-high .496.

And then there's Mike Tauchman, a 27-year-old Rockies outfielder with brief, stale cups of coffee in Colorado. He blew Statcast's Outs Above Average metric out the water, and did it while slugging 13 home runs in half a season of work. (Tauchman got with the program and ended his season on the IL, too.)

When Voit got hurt, 26-year-old rookie Mike Ford did what so many whiff-heavy, older minor-league first baseman do—he brought his impressive Triple-A numbers to the Show, helping ensure the Yankees didn't skip a beat.

Oh, and of course, there's Clint Frazier, a young outfielder who hit real good, fielded real bad and, worst of all, ducked reporters after a few ugly misplays amounted to the worst game of his life. Then, he complained about what he perceived to be unfair media treatment to ESPN's Coley Harvey via text. In fairness to everyone frustrated with him, from beat reporters to Yankees brass, it's much easier to discuss a player's struggles when the player can account for them, as Frazier should have. But, whether it's violence against an intimate partner or parading slurs against blacks and gays on Twitter, all sins can be forgiven—except blaspheming the Holy Press. (Frazier's apparent persona non grata status inside the Yankees organization left him in Triple-A for much of the summer and off the playoff roster.)

And so on.

The impressive stand-ins weren't the only reason the Yankees were good—Brett Gardner went from looking washed to belting a career-high 28 home runs; Masahiro Tanaka and offseason trade acquisition James Paxton were up and down but the former pitched well enough to make his second All-Star team, while the latter finished the season 10-0 with a 2.25 ERA; Aaron Judge missed significant time, worked through an Aaron Judge slump and ended with an Aaron Judge streak; Gary Sánchez bounced back on offense; and the super bullpen, which included a full season of Zack Britton and new signee Adam Ottavino, locked down the game in late innings.

⚾ ⚾ ⚾

If there is a pixie dust capable of turning Quad-A flotsam into 2.7 WARP position players, the dust was gathered with an old Metrocard into fine lines and wantonly snorted throughout the Yankee Stadium front office. But, like a blogger mixing in hackneyed metaphors into his first Baseball Prospectus essay, each one more convoluted than the last, the Yankees got high on their own supply—to the point where they may have acted unwisely.

All these Next Men Up and none—save for 27-year-old Domingo Germán, filling in for Severino—were able to take the ball every fifth day in the rotation. And Germán's ebbs and flows with his fastball velocity, combined with his leap in innings from 2018 (he had a 4.93 ERA from May 24 onward), left him as more of a five-and-dive pitcher, not the guy you'd ideally stack up against Justin Verlander. They were already experimenting with him in long relief before the playoffs, with all those concerns coalescing before a domestic violence allegation ended his season in September.

So, what did the Yankees do at the deadline for an ailing rotation, no certainty that Severino would return healthy, if at all, with Paxton and Tanaka pitching through the worst stretches of their careers? Nothing. They waited on the next man.

The only trade of note Brian Cashman made was for Edwin Encarnación—a proven hitter, but one who did nothing to address their glaring weakness. "The best play was we did nothing," Cashman said moments after the July 31 deadline, in his attempt to deflect criticism about their lack of success pursuing the top-end of the free agent market. He wasn't done inspiring confidence. "We did nothing for a good reason because we felt everything that was in front of me was really not attainable."

(Incidentally, Cashman would later tell Yahoo's Wallace Matthews he doubted Marcus Stroman, who was absolutely attainable, "would be a difference-maker" for their team, adding that the 2019 All-Star would likely fail to crack the Yankees rotation. Stroman was attained by the other New York team, the Mets, with whom he put the finishing touches on a 3.22 ERA/4 WARP season; no Yankees starter crossed 3 WARP.)

Naturally, Cashman was asked about getting outbid for top-flight pitching, like Patrick Corbin, during the previous offseason, to which he told reporters "There's a lot of guys currently sitting in (the Yankees') locker room that wouldn't be here because, again, all that money would have gone in one direction."

You could debate the merits of choosing one dollar versus four quarters, then teaching each scrappy coin about launch angle, but we're not going to legitimize Cashman's false premise that the New York Yankees did not, in fact, have a second dollar bill.

Cashman's inactive deadline didn't matter much during the regular season. The Yankees kept a 103-win pace behind their merry collection of Next Man Ups, from LeMahieu to Tauchman, and by beating the teams in front of them. This is to the players' credit and to the league's shame.

For example, the Yankees went 17-2 against the Orioles. Gleyber Torres hit .394 with 13 of his 38 home runs against a pitching staff that amounted to facing the computer in Triple Play Baseball '99 set to rookie difficulty. It's not his fault, but we all knew he was playing two-player mode with the DualShock controller plugged into the second port—everyone was, really, when it came to facing the Orioles and other tanking teams.

In 2019, four teams won 100-plus games because four teams lost 100-plus games. When planned obsolescence is guiding the long-term strategies of a third of the league, juggernauts just aren't what they used to be. Like 20 home runs, a 4.00 ERA, 200 innings pitched or a 10-strikeout performance, 100 wins is a round number that may be a useful shorthand for excellence in another era. But not ours, not anymore.

When talent is consciously drained from the league, teams like the Yankees can not only hide behind their inaction at the top end of baseball's talent pool—they, and the league, can brand it in the hopes that some fans root for baseball like they're auditioning for a Pirates front office gig. Bob Nutting's not gonna hire you, bro.

The Yankees were fine in the regular season. They were always going to be fine. But, flash forward to the postseason, specifically Game 6 of the ALCS, when Jose Altuve ended a closely contested series with a walk-off home run against Aroldis Chapman, and the Yankees were considerably less fine.

Even though there was supposedly nothing attainable on the starting-pitcher market, except the non-difference-making Stroman, the Yankees probably would've liked a mulligan after losing a planned bullpen game. Relievers like

Britton, echoing comments made by Green, told reporters he felt "uber-exposed" by pitching so frequently, in lieu of high level starters, during a short series. Their top three starters, Tanaka, Paxton and Severino, combined for 23 2/3 innings in their five starts. The Yankees' bullpen-heavy strategy almost worked—their series ERA was 3.13—but they stretched it too far.

"That's why we're relievers, not starters," said Britton. "You overexpose guys, it's inevitable that eventually, they're going to get got a little bit."

As of press time, the Yankees haven't rationalized their premature exit by blaming banging trash cans and espionage. Instead, they signed Gerrit Cole to a nine-year, $324 million contract—the largest length, average annual value and dollar amount awarded to any pitcher ever. Cole offers many luxuries, including the ability to piece together elite production while consistently throwing over 200 innings, a league-wide rarity and function no one on the current staff has shown the capacity for. Slotting Severino, Paxton and Tanaka into the two through four slots gives a playoff rotation few teams can expect to match.

Cole is the ace the Yankees finally decided to splurge on after passing on Stroman, Corbin and others over the past couple deadlines and winters. In a sense, the ultimate next man up.

⚾ ⚾ ⚾

The concept of #NextManUp is unlikely to go away, even after the Yankees behaved like...well, the Yankees. Cashman also allowed mainstays, like Betances and fan-favorite shortstop Didi Gregorius, to walk in free agency. (Didi to the Phillies, Betances to the Mets.) Both players had down years due to injury (or age?) at positions where the Yankees had strong depth, making the moves defensible. Elongated Orioles jokes aside, Gleyber is a stud who looks more comfortable playing his natural position. Meanwhile, Britton, Ottavino, Green, Tommy Kahnle and Chapman—who tacked on another year to his contract after winning the AL Reliever of the Year Award—are perhaps the only set of relievers that could possibly make Betances redundant.

Still, those planned redundancies sustained the Yankees, and enabled them to overcome an absurd rash of injuries in 2019. The Yankees are betting their uncanny and unprecedented injury bug won't return. (They also fired their director of strength and conditioning after six years on the job, so maybe the organization doesn't find it totally uncanny.) If it does, New York might not have the depth to combat the losses now that, as Cashman said, "all that money is going in one direction."

Of course, the Yankees could have kept everyone—such a plan would have complicated their desire to remain under the highest luxury-tax tier, where few teams dare to tread. (As of press time, there were rumors of the Yankees dumping J.A. Happ's contract to reduce their number. Plans can change, so kudos to the

Yankees if they decided to go all-in on leveraging their financial might.) If the Yankees are allowing the tax to drive their roster situations, surprising as it may be to some after making Cole the richest pitcher alive, it would absolutely fit into the team's recent history of permitting external forces to guide their hand.

The Yankees shouldn't rob Peter to pay Paul when they're wealthy enough to keep both around and pay the relative pittance of a luxury tax, even if the 2020 team may be strong enough relative to their peers that it won't matter anyway. But, I don't have a snappy hashtag for that. ■

—Bradford William Davis is an author at the New York Daily News.

Part 2: Player Analysis

PLAYER COMMENTS WITH GRAPHS

Thairo Estrada MI

Born: 02/22/96 Age: 24 Bats: R Throws: R
Height: 5'10" Weight: 190 Origin: International Free Agent, 2012

YEAR	TEAM	LVL	AGE	PA	R	2B	3B	HR	RBI	BB	K	SB	CS	AVG/OBP/SLG
2017	TRN	AA	21	542	72	19	4	6	48	34	56	8	11	.301/.353/.392
2018	TAM	A+	22	47	4	2	0	0	5	0	9	0	0	.222/.234/.267
2018	SWB	AAA	22	34	1	1	0	0	3	0	8	0	0	.152/.176/.182
2019	SWB	AAA	23	259	39	17	2	8	32	14	50	3	1	.266/.313/.452
2019	NYA	MLB	23	69	12	3	0	3	12	3	15	4	0	.250/.294/.438
2020	*NYA*	*MLB*	*24*	*105*	*10*	*5*	*0*	*3*	*11*	*5*	*22*	*1*	*1*	*.236/.280/.373*

Comparables: Yairo Muñoz, Abiatal Avelino, Richard Ureña

After missing most of the 2018 season after being shot during a robbery attempt in Venezuela before spring training, Estrada returned to showcase a truly endearing 25th-man profile. In his MLB debut, Estrada laid down a textbook sacrifice bunt as a pinch hitter. A week later, the natural infielder started in left. Estrada's an athlete who will give you whatever you need from him—as long as you don't need him to do it with flare or stand out in any particular way. Come up big with bases loaded? He's got you. Learn a new position in three days? He's got you. This guy just delivers in the most W.B. Mason style possible. You know, a few cases of Keurig cups here, a few boxes of pens there and maybe even the occasional 50-pound bag of rock salt for those front steps.

YEAR	TEAM	LVL	AGE	PA	DRC+	VORP	BABIP	BRR	FRAA	WARP
2017	TRN	AA	21	542	117	32.7	.327	-2.2	SS(90): -0.3, 2B(23): -0.5	2.8
2018	TAM	A+	22	47	48	-2.9	.270	-0.6	SS(8): -0.2	-0.2
2018	SWB	AAA	22	34	20	-3.9	.200	-0.3	SS(5): 0.0, 2B(3): 0.9	-0.1
2019	SWB	AAA	23	259	86	4.0	.304	-1.1	SS(32): 1.7, 2B(24): -0.9	0.5
2019	NYA	MLB	23	69	87	1.3	.283	1.0	2B(17): -1.1, SS(9): 0.3	0.1
2020	*NYA*	*MLB*	*24*	*105*	*75*	*0.5*	*.276*	*-0.2*	*SS 0, 2B -1*	*0.0*

Thairo Estrada, continued

Batted Ball Distribution

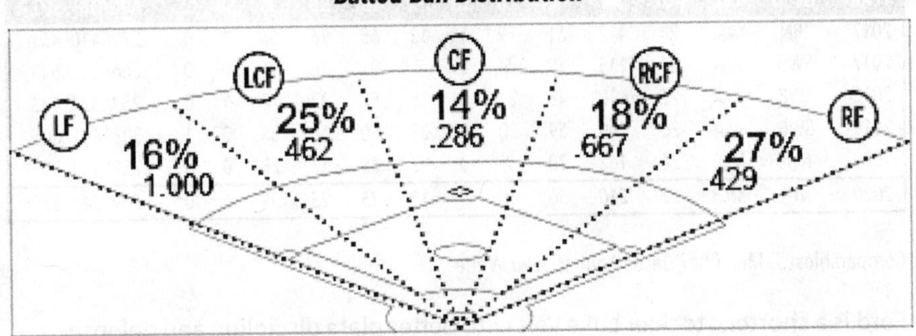

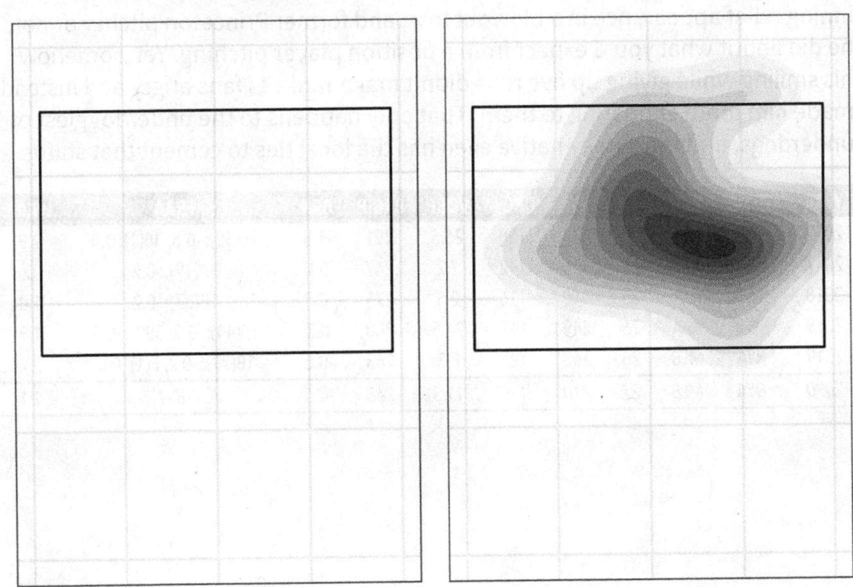

Mike Ford 1B

Born: 07/04/92 Age: 27 Bats: L Throws: R
Height: 6'0" Weight: 225 Origin: Undrafted Free Agent, 2013

YEAR	TEAM	LVL	AGE	PA	R	2B	3B	HR	RBI	BB	K	SB	CS	AVG/OBP/SLG
2017	TRN	AA	24	417	61	19	1	13	65	76	56	1	0	.272/.410/.451
2017	SWB	AAA	24	115	19	5	0	7	21	18	16	0	0	.266/.383/.543
2018	SWB	AAA	25	410	48	21	0	15	52	37	70	1	0	.253/.327/.433
2019	SWB	AAA	26	349	59	20	0	23	60	46	55	0	1	.303/.401/.605
2019	NYA	MLB	26	163	30	7	0	12	25	17	28	0	0	.259/.350/.559
2020	*NYA*	*MLB*	*27*	*210*	*30*	*10*	*0*	*13*	*35*	*23*	*39*	*0*	*0*	*.259/.346/.525*

Comparables: Ji-Man Choi, Jesús Aguilar, Tyler White

Ford is a shorter, stockier Luke Voit with better plate discipline and defense around the cold corner. He doesn't have the “wow” factor of his counterpart and lacks similar power, but there's a lot to like about his approach, and the fact that he's left-handed certainly doesn't hurt at Yankee Stadium. He made a two-inning relief appearance in a blowout loss, and former Princeton pitcher or not, he did about what you'd expect from a position player pitching. Yet, somehow his smiling while giving up five runs didn't make Yankees fans angry and instead made him more endearing to them. That only happens to the underdoggiest of underdogs, and the Jersey native even has the local ties to cement that status.

YEAR	TEAM	LVL	AGE	PA	DRC+	VORP	BABIP	BRR	FRAA	WARP
2017	TRN	AA	24	417	158	26.5	.291	-1.8	1B(55): -0.5, 3B(1): 0.0	2.9
2017	SWB	AAA	24	115	142	7.2	.247	0.1	1B(19): -0.2	0.6
2018	SWB	AAA	25	410	116	2.5	.275	-0.9	1B(57): -0.2	1.0
2019	SWB	AAA	26	349	141	24.5	.300	0.3	1B(44): -3.2, 3B(5): 0.0	1.8
2019	NYA	MLB	26	163	125	8.3	.243	-0.6	1B(29): -0.2, P(1): 0.0	0.7
2020	*NYA*	*MLB*	*27*	*210*	*130*	*11.3*	*.263*	*-0.5*	*1B -1*	*1.1*

Mike Ford, continued

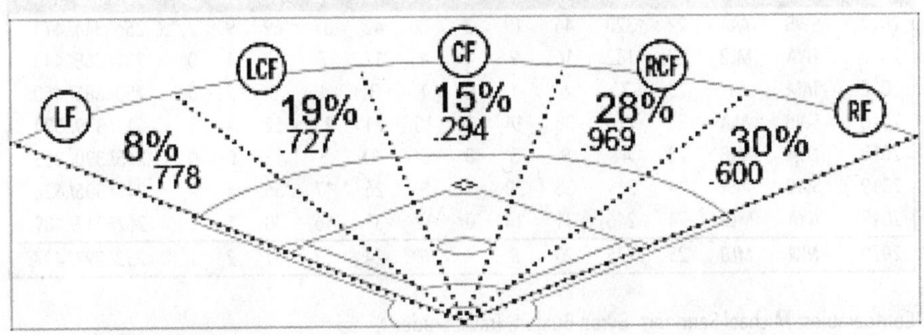

Strike Zone vs LHP | **Strike Zone vs RHP**

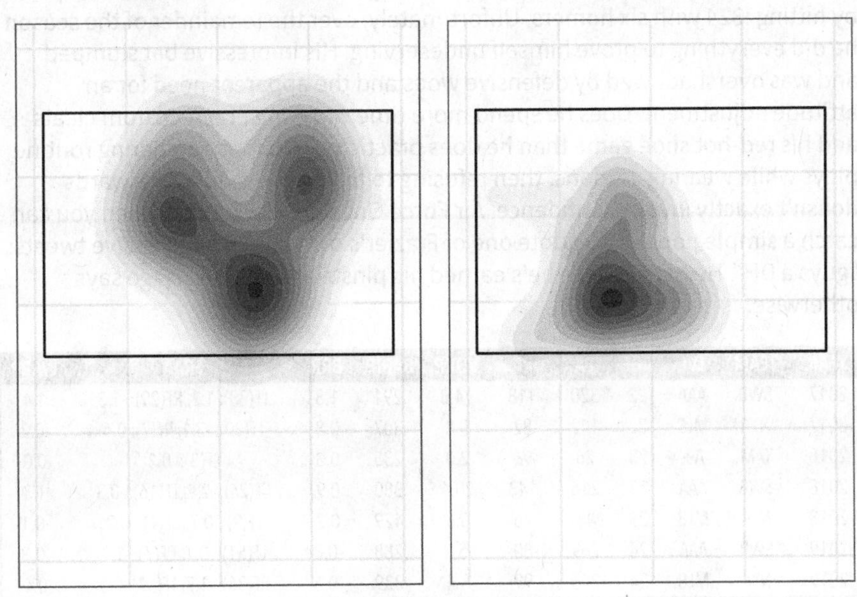

Clint Frazier OF

Born: 09/06/94 Age: 25 Bats: R Throws: R
Height: 6'1" Weight: 190 Origin: Round 1, 2013 Draft (#5 overall)

YEAR	TEAM	LVL	AGE	PA	R	2B	3B	HR	RBI	BB	K	SB	CS	AVG/OBP/SLG
2017	SWB	AAA	22	320	46	19	2	12	42	37	69	9	2	.256/.344/.473
2017	NYA	MLB	22	142	16	9	4	4	17	7	43	1	0	.231/.268/.448
2018	TAM	A+	23	26	6	1	0	1	3	4	3	2	0	.250/.385/.450
2018	SWB	AAA	23	216	38	14	3	10	21	23	52	4	2	.311/.389/.574
2018	NYA	MLB	23	41	9	3	0	0	1	5	13	0	0	.265/.390/.353
2019	SWB	AAA	24	269	35	20	1	8	26	17	56	1	2	.247/.305/.433
2019	NYA	MLB	24	246	31	14	0	12	38	16	70	1	2	.267/.317/.489
2020	*NYA*	*MLB*	*25*	*175*	*20*	*8*	*1*	*8*	*24*	*13*	*51*	*2*	*1*	*.233/.297/.437*

Comparables: Michael Saunders, Byron Buxton, Travis Snider

Frazier opened the year declaring he was gunning for a starting job, then proceeded to show off his lumber while filling in for Giancarlo Stanton in April by hitting .324 with six homers. Unfortunately, over the remainder of the season he did everything to prove himself undeserving. His impressive bat slumped and was overshadowed by defensive woes and the apparent need for an attitude adjustment. Does he spend more time worrying about custom cleats and his red-hot shoe game than he does practicing? No. But butchering routine plays while wearing Jordans, then refusing to talk to the media afterwards doesn't exactly invoke confidence. Air Force Ones only look good when you can catch a simple pop up. To quote one of Frazier's own passive-aggressive tweets: “guys a DH”. He may believe he's earned his pinstripes, but his usage says otherwise.

YEAR	TEAM	LVL	AGE	PA	DRC+	VORP	BABIP	BRR	FRAA	WARP
2017	SWB	AAA	22	320	118	14.8	.291	1.8	LF(38): 1.2, RF(29): -1.3	1.4
2017	NYA	MLB	22	142	82	0.8	.307	0.8	LF(30): -3.1, RF(7): 0.4	-0.2
2018	TAM	A+	23	26	96	2.0	.235	0.3	LF(3): -0.3	0.0
2018	SWB	AAA	23	216	143	20.4	.380	0.9	CF(26): -2.9, LF(16): -0.3	1.3
2018	NYA	MLB	23	41	76	0.6	.429	0.2	LF(9): -0.7, CF(1): -0.2	-0.1
2019	SWB	AAA	24	269	80	-5.2	.288	-0.8	LF(51): -0.1, CF(7): -1.3	-0.2
2019	NYA	MLB	24	246	99	5.4	.329	-0.6	RF(36): -1.7, LF(17): 0.5	0.4
2020	*NYA*	*MLB*	*25*	*175*	*94*	*2.7*	*.291*	*0.2*	*LF -1, RF 0*	*0.1*

Clint Frazier, continued

Batted Ball Distribution

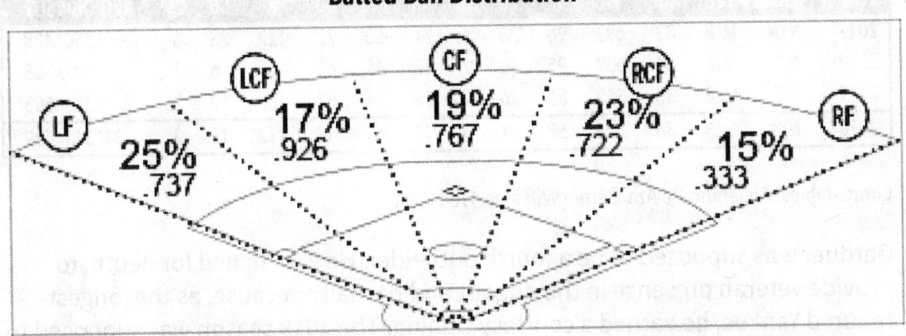

Strike Zone vs LHP

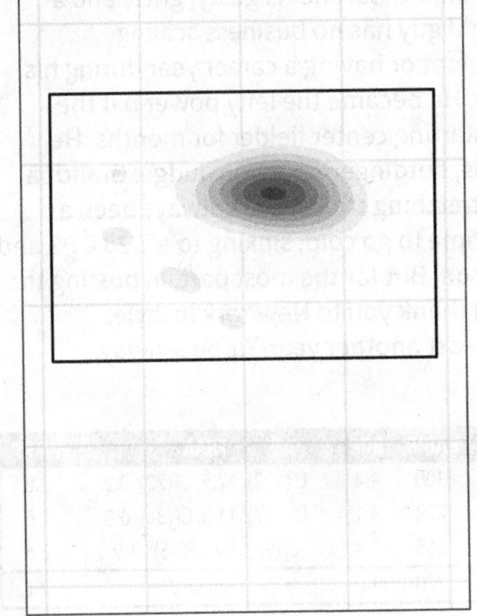

Strike Zone vs RHP

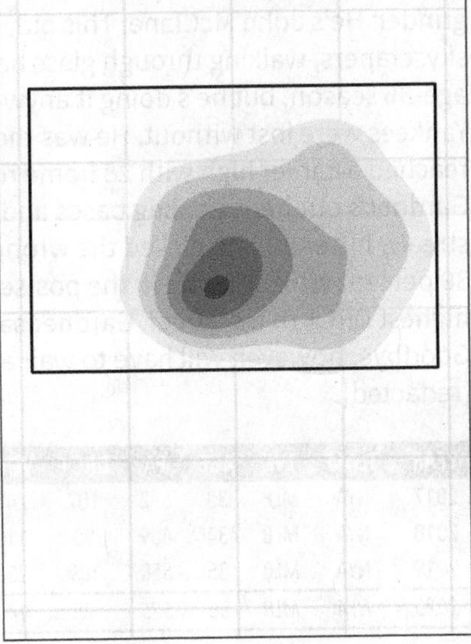

Brett Gardner OF

Born: 08/24/83 Age: 36 Bats: L Throws: L
Height: 5'11" Weight: 195 Origin: Round 3, 2005 Draft (#109 overall)

YEAR	TEAM	LVL	AGE	PA	R	2B	3B	HR	RBI	BB	K	SB	CS	AVG/OBP/SLG
2017	NYA	MLB	33	682	96	26	4	21	63	72	122	23	5	.264/.350/.428
2018	NYA	MLB	34	609	95	20	7	12	45	65	107	16	2	.236/.322/.368
2019	NYA	MLB	35	550	86	26	7	28	74	52	108	10	2	.251/.325/.503
2020	*NYA*	*MLB*	*36*	*525*	*59*	*21*	*3*	*18*	*63*	*49*	*112*	*12*	*3*	*.234/.313/.409*

Comparables: Alejandro De Aza, Bernie Williams, Fred Lynn

Gardner was supposed to be a fourth outfielder. He was signed for depth, to provide veteran presence in the dugout and partially because, as the longest-tenured Yankee, he earned a courtesy signing. The 2019 season was supposed to mark a turning point in Gardner's career where he'd pass the torch onto the next batch of hopeful prospects. He'd come in as a late inning defensive replacement and share war stories about life before they let iPads in the dugouts. A lot was supposed to happen this season, and it didn't. Gardner is gusty, gritty and a grinder. He's John McClane. This old, bald guy has no business scaling skyscrapers, walking through glass barefoot or having a career year during his age-36 season, but he's doing it anyway. He became the lefty power bat the Yankees were lost without. He was the starting center fielder for months. He reached a career high with 28 home runs, outdingering Aaron Judge. Grandpa Gardner's out here stealing bases and stretching triples. He's always been a streaky hitter and he picked the wrong time to go cold, sinking to a .528 OPS and 39 percent strikeout rate in the postseason. But for the most part, in posting the highest DRC+ of his career, Gardner said thank you to New York in style. Goodbye, however, will have to wait at least another year. Yippee-ki-yay, [redacted].

YEAR	TEAM	LVL	AGE	PA	DRC+	VORP	BABIP	BRR	FRAA	WARP
2017	NYA	MLB	33	682	107	24.4	.300	1.4	LF(122): 12.5, CF(22): 0.2	3.8
2018	NYA	MLB	34	609	90	11.9	.272	4.1	LF(107): 11.8, CF(34): 0.0	2.6
2019	NYA	MLB	35	550	109	25.9	.265	1.4	CF(98): 1.7, LF(45): -1.9	2.6
2020	*NYA*	*MLB*	*36*	*525*	*95*	*14.2*	*.270*	*1.0*	*LF 6, CF 0*	*2.1*

Brett Gardner, continued

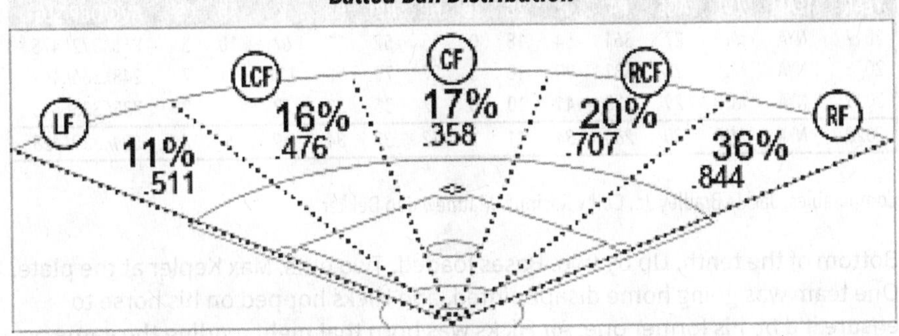

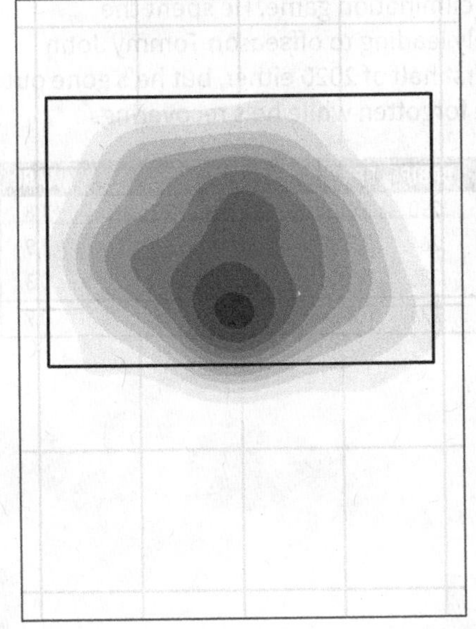

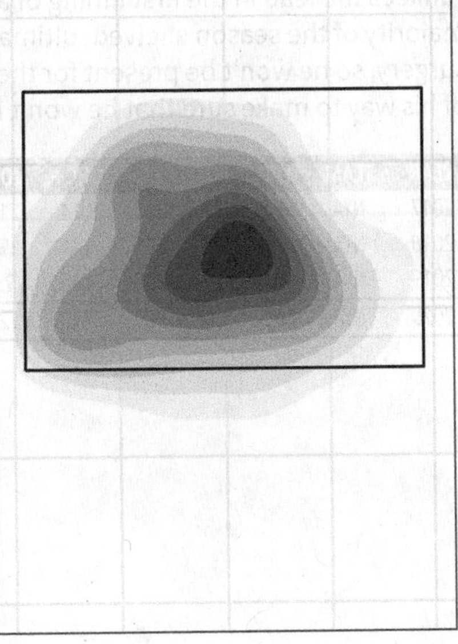

Aaron Hicks CF

Born: 10/02/89 Age: 30 Bats: B Throws: R
Height: 6'1" Weight: 202 Origin: Round 1, 2008 Draft (#14 overall)

YEAR	TEAM	LVL	AGE	PA	R	2B	3B	HR	RBI	BB	K	SB	CS	AVG/OBP/SLG
2017	NYA	MLB	27	361	54	18	0	15	52	51	67	10	5	.266/.372/.475
2018	NYA	MLB	28	581	90	18	3	27	79	90	111	11	2	.248/.366/.467
2019	NYA	MLB	29	255	41	10	0	12	36	31	72	1	2	.235/.325/.443
2020	*NYA*	*MLB*	*30*	*280*	*34*	*11*	*1*	*12*	*37*	*34*	*69*	*5*	*2*	*.234/.330/.428*

Comparables: Jackie Bradley Jr., Colby Rasmus, Matthew den Dekker

Bottom of the tenth. Up by two. Bases loaded. Two outs. Max Kepler at the plate. One team was going home disappointed, and Hicks hopped on his horse to ensure it'd be his former one. Air Hicks was born that night, ending the game on the flashiest of plays and justifying his contract extension with one diving catch. On the other side of the ball, months later, Hicks mashed a highlight reel home run off of Cy Young winner Justin Verlander in Game 5 of the ALCS, giving the Yankees the lead in the first inning of an elimination game. He spent the majority of the season shelved, ultimately leading to offseason Tommy John surgery, so he won't be present for the first half of 2020 either, but he's gone out of his way to make sure that he won't be forgotten while he's recovering.

YEAR	TEAM	LVL	AGE	PA	DRC+	VORP	BABIP	BRR	FRAA	WARP
2017	NYA	MLB	27	361	114	21.2	.290	2.0	CF(52): -0.8, LF(22): 0.8	1.8
2018	NYA	MLB	28	581	121	35.9	.264	2.3	CF(131): -8.6	2.9
2019	NYA	MLB	29	255	100	9.4	.286	0.3	CF(58): -6.8	0.3
2020	*NYA*	*MLB*	*30*	*280*	*105*	*12.9*	*.278*	*0.8*	*CF -4*	*0.9*

Aaron Hicks, continued

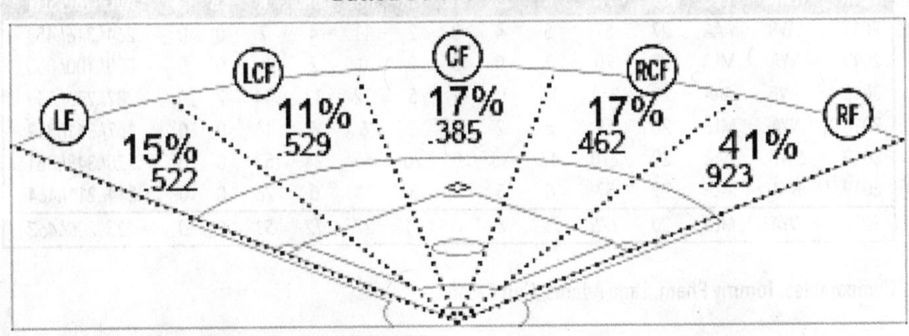

Strike Zone vs LHP

Strike Zone vs RHP

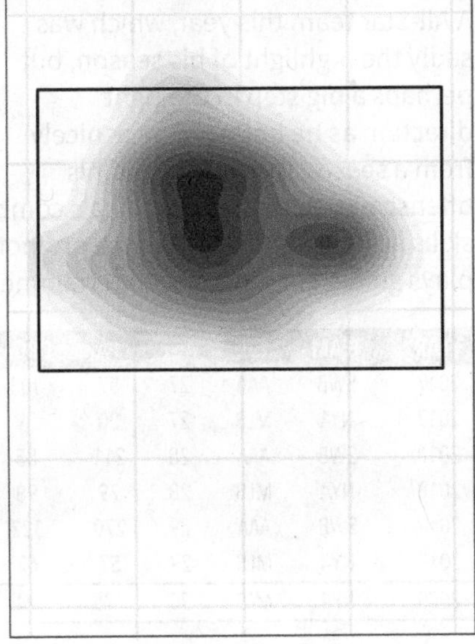

Kyle Higashioka C

Born: 04/20/90 Age: 30 Bats: R Throws: R
Height: 6'1" Weight: 205 Origin: Round 7, 2008 Draft (#230 overall)

YEAR	TEAM	LVL	AGE	PA	R	2B	3B	HR	RBI	BB	K	SB	CS	AVG/OBP/SLG
2017	SWB	AAA	27	57	5	4	0	2	11	4	7	0	0	.264/.316/.453
2017	NYA	MLB	27	20	2	0	0	0	0	2	6	0	0	.000/.100/.000
2018	SWB	AAA	28	211	16	10	1	5	22	17	44	2	0	.202/.276/.346
2018	NYA	MLB	28	79	6	2	0	3	6	6	16	0	0	.167/.241/.319
2019	SWB	AAA	29	270	42	13	0	20	56	24	53	0	0	.278/.348/.581
2019	NYA	MLB	29	57	8	5	0	3	11	0	26	0	0	.214/.211/.464
2020	*NYA*	*MLB*	*30*	*175*	*22*	*6*	*0*	*11*	*27*	*12*	*51*	*0*	*0*	*.223/.280/.462*

Comparables: Tommy Pham, Lane Adams, Curt Casali

YEAR	TEAM	P. COUNT	FRM RUNS	BLK RUNS	THRW RUNS	TOT RUNS
2017	NYA	813	1.7	-0.1	0.0	1.5
2017	SWB	2153	4.3	-0.3	-0.1	3.8
2018	NYA	3384	3.2	0.8	-0.1	4.4
2018	SWB	6908	7.2	0.6	-0.2	7.6
2019	NYA	2271	1.9	0.1	-0.1	1.7
2019	SWB	8880	15.4	0.0	-0.1	15.1
2020	*NYA*	*6833*	*7.8*	*0.3*	*-0.1*	*8.0*

The backup to the backup, Higashioka's time in the big leagues has been contingent on Gary Sánchez's health. He made the Triple-A All-Star team this year, which was sadly the highlight of his season, but perhaps a big step in the right direction as he bounced back nicely from a season that undersold his offensive potential. Higashioka's combination of power and strong receiving skills are enough to earn him a promotion to a singular understudy role. He also plays guitar, so rain delay entertainment is always at his fingertips.

YEAR	TEAM	LVL	AGE	PA	DRC+	VORP	BABIP	BRR	FRAA	WARP
2017	SWB	AAA	27	57	103	2.2	.273	-0.2	C(14): 4.5	0.7
2017	NYA	MLB	27	20	59	-1.7	.000	-0.1	C(8): 1.6	0.2
2018	SWB	AAA	28	211	55	-0.9	.234	-0.7	C(49): 6.6	0.6
2018	NYA	MLB	28	79	98	-2.6	.170	-0.7	C(27): 3.8	0.7
2019	SWB	AAA	29	270	122	19.1	.276	-3.2	C(64): 15.2	3.0
2019	NYA	MLB	29	57	62	0.2	.321	0.6	C(18): 2.1	0.3
2020	*NYA*	*MLB*	*30*	*175*	*94*	*6.4*	*.254*	*-0.4*	*C 8*	*1.5*

Kyle Higashioka, continued

Batted Ball Distribution

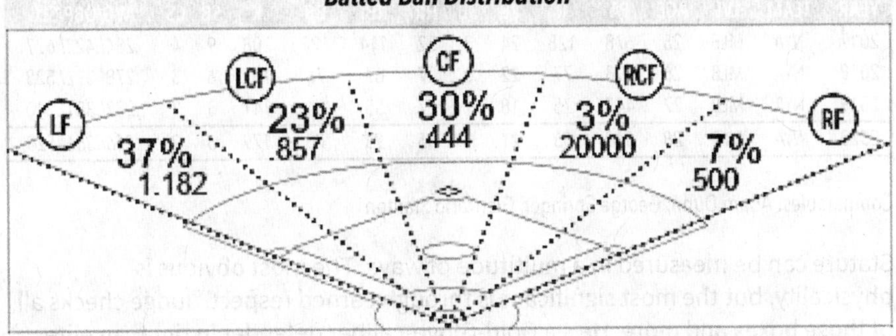

Strike Zone vs LHP

Strike Zone vs RHP

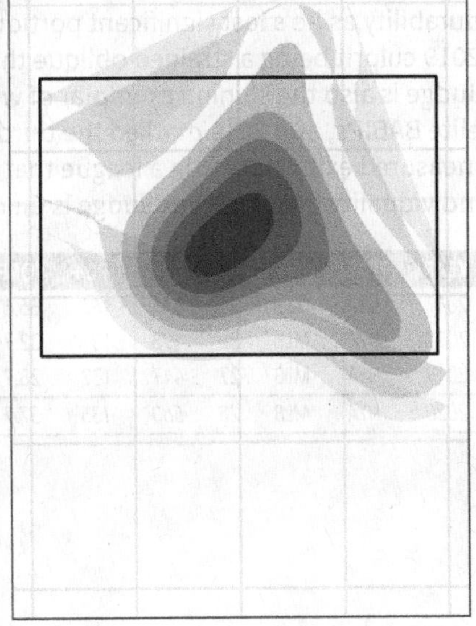

Aaron Judge RF

Born: 04/26/92 Age: 28 Bats: R Throws: R
Height: 6'7" Weight: 282 Origin: Round 1, 2013 Draft (#32 overall)

YEAR	TEAM	LVL	AGE	PA	R	2B	3B	HR	RBI	BB	K	SB	CS	AVG/OBP/SLG
2017	NYA	MLB	25	678	128	24	3	52	114	127	208	9	4	.284/.422/.627
2018	NYA	MLB	26	498	77	22	0	27	67	76	152	6	3	.278/.392/.528
2019	NYA	MLB	27	447	75	18	1	27	55	64	141	3	2	.272/.381/.540
2020	*NYA*	*MLB*	*28*	*560*	*83*	*21*	*1*	*35*	*93*	*78*	*179*	*6*	*2*	*.256/.366/.523*

Comparables: Adam Dunn, George Springer, Giancarlo Stanton

Stature can be measured in a multitude of ways. The most obvious is physicality, but the most significant is through earned respect. Judge checks all of those boxes and more: He's a Gold-Glove-caliber defender in right, an elite slugger, even potentially the new captain in the Bronx. He's one of just a handful of players in baseball who is recognizable off the field and has single-handedly driven up usage of the number 99 in youth baseball and softball leagues across the Tri-State Area by roughly 2000% (probably). Well, all of the boxes except for durability as he's lost significant portions of each of the last two seasons—the 2019 culprit being a strained oblique that cost him much of May and June. Judge is also the shining exemplar of why you don't need to be fast to put up elite BABIPs, and 2019 marked the third season in a row leading all of baseball in measured exit velocity. In a league that seemingly enjoys stamping out of the individuality of its players, Judge is uniquely...well, unique.

YEAR	TEAM	LVL	AGE	PA	DRC+	VORP	BABIP	BRR	FRAA	WARP
2017	NYA	MLB	25	678	166	66.6	.357	-0.1	RF(141): 4.4	7.5
2018	NYA	MLB	26	498	137	32.7	.368	1.0	RF(90): 12.6, CF(1): -0.1	4.7
2019	NYA	MLB	27	447	132	28.7	.360	0.2	RF(92): 8.3	3.6
2020	*NYA*	*MLB*	*28*	*560*	*135*	*37.7*	*.332*	*0.5*	*RF 6*	*4.6*

Aaron Judge, continued

Batted Ball Distribution

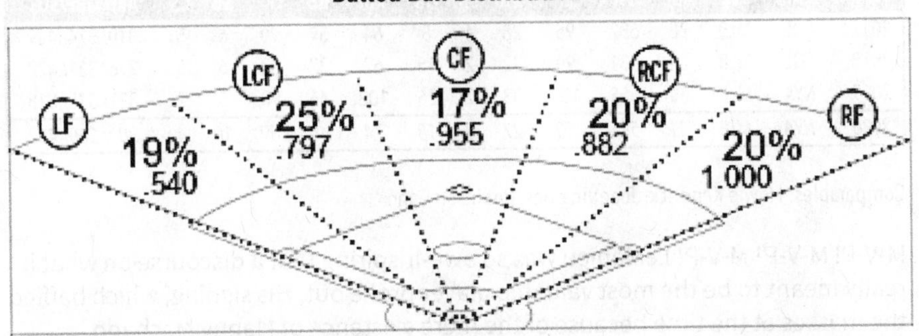

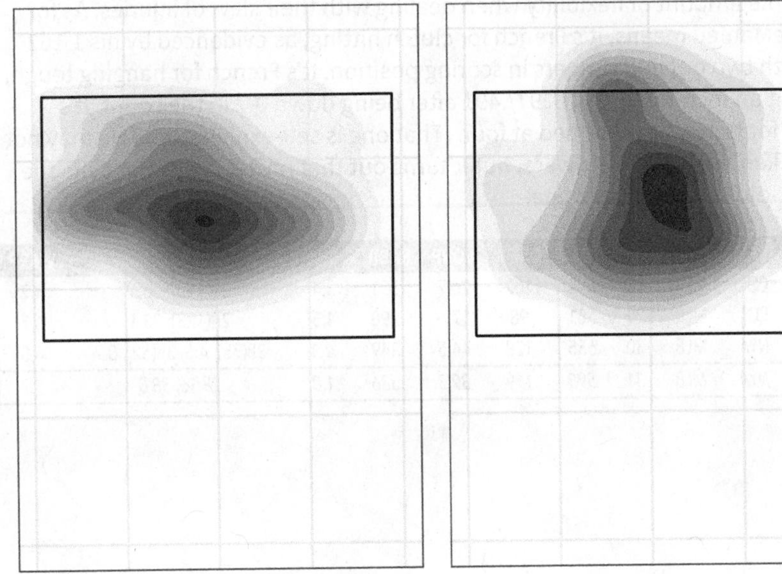

DJ LeMahieu 2B

Born: 07/13/88 Age: 31 Bats: R Throws: R
Height: 6'4" Weight: 215 Origin: Round 2, 2009 Draft (#79 overall)

YEAR	TEAM	LVL	AGE	PA	R	2B	3B	HR	RBI	BB	K	SB	CS	AVG/OBP/SLG
2017	COL	MLB	28	682	95	28	4	8	64	59	90	6	5	.310/.374/.409
2018	COL	MLB	29	581	90	32	2	15	62	37	82	6	5	.276/.321/.428
2019	NYA	MLB	30	655	109	33	2	26	102	46	90	5	2	.327/.375/.518
2020	*NYA*	*MLB*	*31*	*595*	*70*	*27*	*3*	*18*	*74*	*46*	*89*	*10*	*4*	*.303/.360/.462*

Comparables: Howie Kendrick, Joaquin Arias, Robinson Canó

M-V-P! M-V-P! M-V-P! LeMahieu was so awe-inspiring that a discourse on what it really meant to be the most valuable player broke out. His signing, which baffled the masses at the time because of the mere existence of Manny Machado, turned out to be the gift that keeps on giving. A calm and unshakable demeanor was the perfect addition to a pressure-filled New York team, and his ability to play three infield positions at an above-average level gave the Yankees an incredible amount of flexibility when dealing with their slew of injuries. As for what LeMahieu means, it's French for clutch hitting, as evidenced by his 1.162 OPS with two out and runners in scoring position. It's French for hanging tough, as he hit an incredible .274/.297/.491 after being down 0-2 in the count. It's French for holy shit we're tied at four. (That one is self-explanatory.) He may not have taken home the hardware, but it turns out that niveau de la mer suits the 31-year-old sparkplug just fine.

YEAR	TEAM	LVL	AGE	PA	DRC+	VORP	BABIP	BRR	FRAA	WARP
2017	COL	MLB	28	682	102	26.7	.351	3.4	2B(153): 20.5	4.7
2018	COL	MLB	29	581	98	17.6	.298	4.5	2B(128): 20.1	4.2
2019	NYA	MLB	30	655	128	44.5	.349	-2.1	2B(75): 4.5, 3B(52): 0.7	4.8
2020	*NYA*	*MLB*	*31*	*595*	*119*	*39.3*	*.336*	*1.8*	*2B 16, 3B 0*	*5.7*

DJ LeMahieu, continued

Batted Ball Distribution

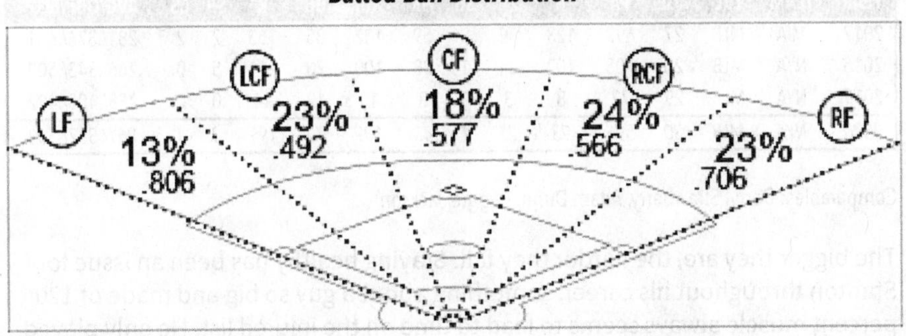

Strike Zone vs LHP

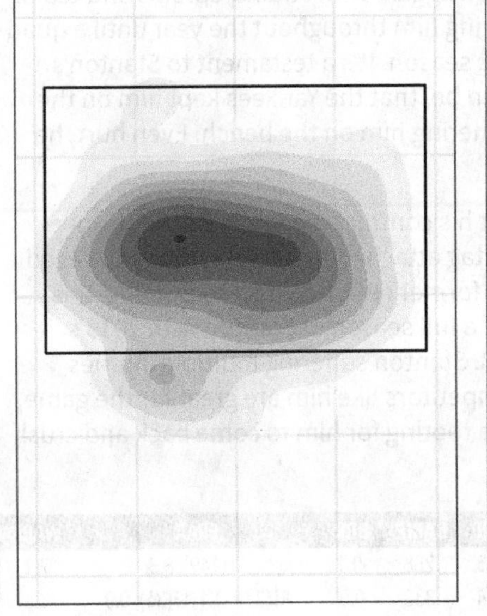

Strike Zone vs RHP

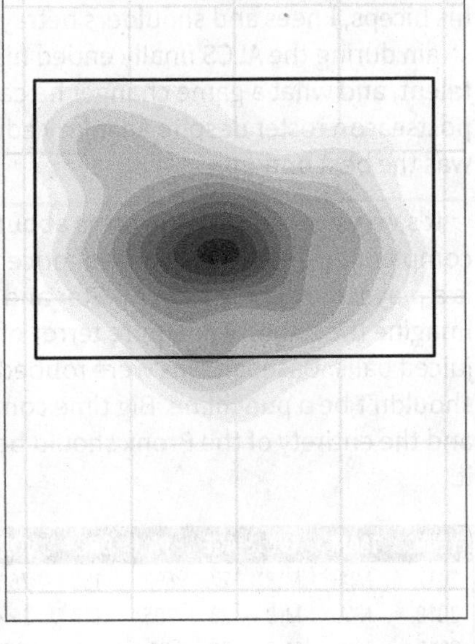

Giancarlo Stanton OF

Born: 11/08/89 Age: 30 Bats: R Throws: R
Height: 6'6" Weight: 245 Origin: Round 2, 2007 Draft (#76 overall)

YEAR	TEAM	LVL	AGE	PA	R	2B	3B	HR	RBI	BB	K	SB	CS	AVG/OBP/SLG
2017	MIA	MLB	27	692	123	32	0	59	132	85	163	2	2	.281/.376/.631
2018	NYA	MLB	28	705	102	34	1	38	100	70	211	5	0	.266/.343/.509
2019	NYA	MLB	29	72	8	3	0	3	13	12	24	0	0	.288/.403/.492
2020	*NYA*	*MLB*	*30*	*595*	*93*	*25*	*1*	*43*	*109*	*72*	*191*	*3*	*1*	*.261/.357/.563*

Comparables: Darryl Strawberry, Adam Dunn, Reggie Jackson

The bigger they are, the harder they fall. Staying healthy has been an issue for Stanton throughout his career, something about a guy so big and made of 120 percent muscle always seems to lead to time on the injured list. He only played in 23 games, including the postseason, and despite what irrationally angry Yankees fans think they know, no one was more frustrated by that than Stanton himself. His road to recovery was equally frustrating. When he solved one injury, three more popped up in its place. He struggled with strains, sprains and tears; his biceps, knees and shoulders betraying him throughout the year until a quad strain during the ALCS finally ended his season. It's a testament to Stanton's talent, and what a game changer he can be, that the Yankees kept him on the postseason roster despite an injury adhering him on the bench. Even hurt, he was the best option.

It's very easy to get up in arms about his contract, and boy do people love complaining about every type of price tag attached to him. But the real tragedy is a player like Stanton, an All-Star and former MVP, having a season like this. Imagine the majesty and pure terror of a full season of Stanton with 2019's juiced balls. Baseball fans were robbed. Stanton suffering multiple injuries shouldn't be a punchline. Big time competitors like him are great for the game, and the entirety of the Bronx should be rooting for him to come back and crush it.

YEAR	TEAM	LVL	AGE	PA	DRC+	VORP	BABIP	BRR	FRAA	WARP
2017	MIA	MLB	27	692	155	76.5	.288	-0.1	RF(149): 8.3	7.1
2018	NYA	MLB	28	705	117	29.4	.333	0.0	RF(37): -1.1, LF(36): 0.0	2.6
2019	NYA	MLB	29	72	87	0.5	.424	-0.3	LF(10): -1.3, RF(3): -0.4	-0.2
2020	*NYA*	*MLB*	*30*	*595*	*141*	*43.2*	*.324*	*-0.3*	*LF -5, RF 0*	*4.0*

Giancarlo Stanton, continued

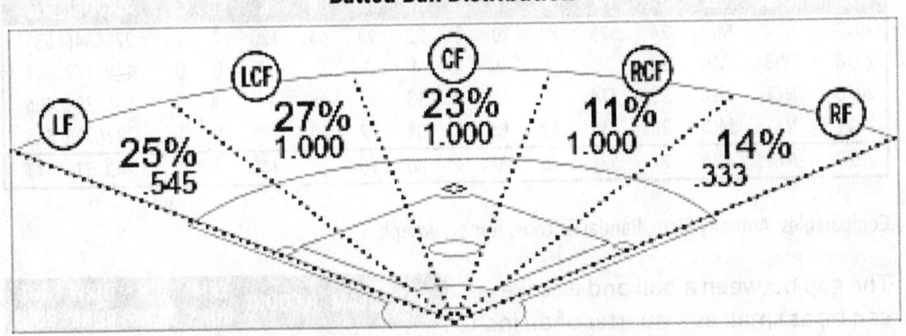

Strike Zone vs LHP

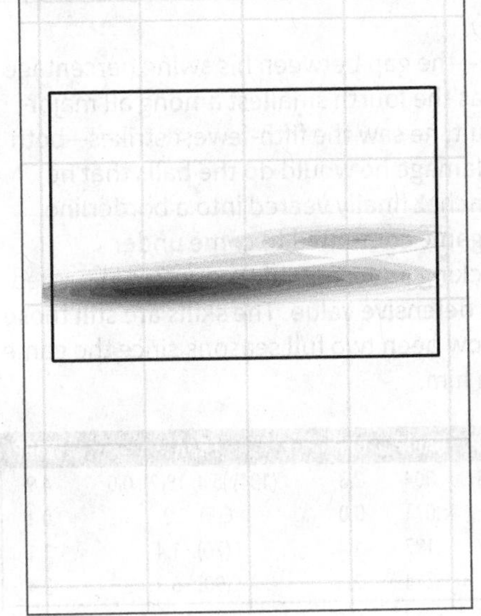

Strike Zone vs RHP

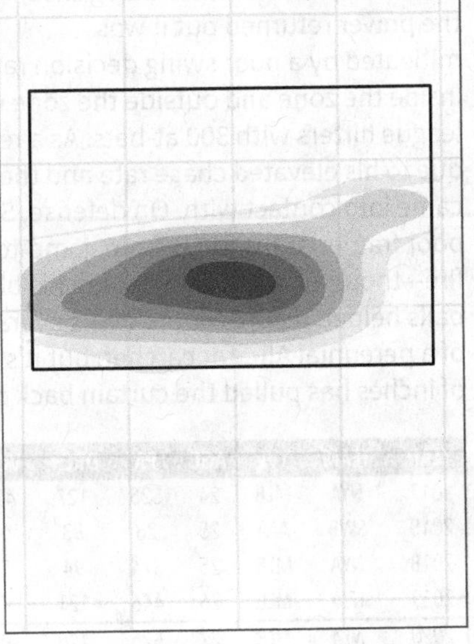

Gary Sánchez C

Born: 12/02/92 Age: 27 Bats: R Throws: R
Height: 6'2" Weight: 230 Origin: International Free Agent, 2009

YEAR	TEAM	LVL	AGE	PA	R	2B	3B	HR	RBI	BB	K	SB	CS	AVG/OBP/SLG
2017	NYA	MLB	24	525	79	20	0	33	90	40	120	2	1	.278/.345/.531
2018	SWB	AAA	25	28	4	0	0	4	4	0	10	0	0	.179/.179/.607
2018	NYA	MLB	25	374	51	17	0	18	53	46	94	1	0	.186/.291/.406
2019	NYA	MLB	26	446	62	12	1	34	77	40	125	0	1	.232/.316/.525
2020	*NYA*	*MLB*	*27*	*525*	*75*	*20*	*1*	*36*	*90*	*46*	*140*	*3*	*1*	*.240/.316/.515*

Comparables: Anthony Rizzo, Randal Grichuk, Tommy Joseph

YEAR	TEAM	P. COUNT	FRM RUNS	BLK RUNS	THRW RUNS	TOT RUNS
2017	NYA	14363	7.4	-3.1	2.3	7.2
2018	NYA	10822	3.3	-4.3	0.2	-1.0
2019	NYA	12670	-5.1	-0.8	-0.2	-6.1
2020	*NYA*	*18452*	*2.8*	*-2.3*	*-0.2*	*0.3*

The gap between a ball and a strike can be as small as a quarter of an inch or as large as a couple of wins, and Sánchez was guilty of letting that differentiation hold him back on both sides of the ball in 2019. On offense, the power returned but it was mitigated by a poor swing decision rate—the gap between his swing percentage inside the zone and outside the zone was the fourth smallest among all major-league hitters with 300 at-bats. As a result, he saw the fifth-fewest strikes—both due to his elevated chase rate and the damage he would do the balls that he came into contact with. On defense, Sánchez finally veered into a borderline poor framer as his focus from game-to-game continued to come under fire—though an improvement in his blocking and a notable reduction in passed balls helped recover some of his overall defensive value. The skills are still those of a perennial All-Star catcher, but it's now been two full seasons since the game of inches has pulled the curtain back on him.

YEAR	TEAM	LVL	AGE	PA	DRC+	VORP	BABIP	BRR	FRAA	WARP
2017	NYA	MLB	24	525	127	43.8	.304	2.3	C(104): 5.4, 1B(2): 0.0	4.9
2018	SWB	AAA	25	28	83	0.3	.071	0.0	C(5): 0.0	0.1
2018	NYA	MLB	25	374	94	5.4	.197	-1.4	C(76): -1.4	1.1
2019	NYA	MLB	26	446	121	33.6	.244	-2.5	C(90): -6.3	2.4
2020	*NYA*	*MLB*	*27*	*525*	*118*	*35.3*	*.260*	*-0.4*	*C-1*	*3.6*

Gary Sánchez, continued

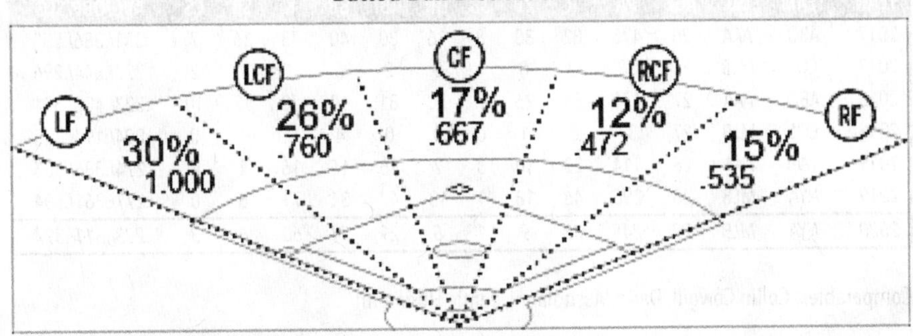

Strike Zone vs LHP

Strike Zone vs RHP

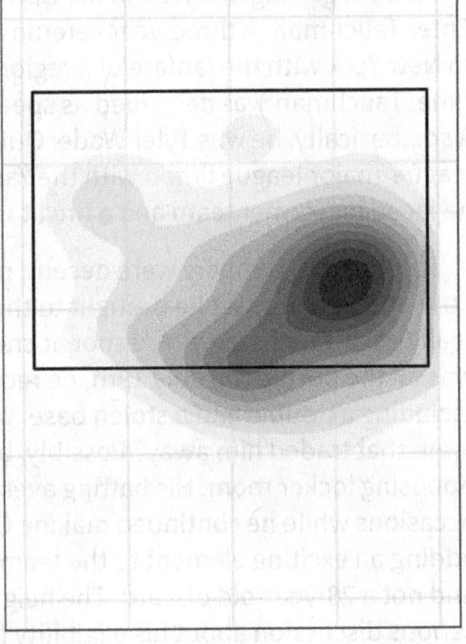

Mike Tauchman OF

Born: 12/03/90 Age: 29 Bats: L Throws: L
Height: 6'2" Weight: 220 Origin: Round 10, 2013 Draft (#289 overall)

YEAR	TEAM	LVL	AGE	PA	R	2B	3B	HR	RBI	BB	K	SB	CS	AVG/OBP/SLG
2017	ABQ	AAA	26	475	82	30	8	16	80	40	73	16	7	.331/.386/.555
2017	COL	MLB	26	32	2	0	1	0	2	5	10	1	2	.222/.344/.296
2018	ABQ	AAA	27	471	84	26	7	20	81	60	70	12	10	.323/.408/.571
2018	COL	MLB	27	37	5	1	0	0	0	4	15	1	0	.094/.194/.125
2019	SWB	AAA	28	114	22	10	3	2	16	16	16	4	0	.274/.386/.505
2019	NYA	MLB	28	296	46	18	1	13	47	34	71	6	0	.277/.361/.504
2020	*NYA*	*MLB*	*29*	*245*	*27*	*9*	*1*	*8*	*29*	*24*	*60*	*6*	*3*	*.233/.311/.397*

Comparables: Collin Cowgill, Darin Mastroianni, Jamie Hoffmann

Aside from maybe Gio Urshela, no player benefited from the historic Yankee injury parade more than Tauchman. When Aaron Hicks hit the injured list before the start of the season, suddenly the outfield depth that supposedly prevented them from getting involved in the Bryce Harper sweepstakes didn't feel so deep. Enter Tauchman. A three-year veteran of the International League, he came over to New York with the fanfare of a regional theater actor trying to make the big time. Tauchman was described as speedy with a great glove who raked in Triple-A so...basically, he was Tyler Wade: Outfield Version. Tauchman lived in minor league/major league limbo with the Yankees, much like he did in Colorado, until he faced his former team and a fire lit under him.

Tauchman's numbers were decent, not great, but his glove was worth what little offensive impact he brought to the table. Playing the Rockies, who never really gave Tauchman a true shot at cracking their roster, set him off. Maybe it was all the purple. On July 19th, he recorded his first three hit game of the year, including a double and a stolen base. Was he simply overperforming against the team that traded him away? Possibly, but it continued long after they left the opposing locker room. His batting average climbed over .300 on multiple occasions while he continued making Gold-Glove-worthy plays in left field, adding an exciting element to the team as if he were a touted outfield prospect and not a 28-year-old discard. The height of Tauchman's season involved some serious discussion about his eligibility for Rookie of the Year and minor outrage when it was revealed he was not. Tauchman made the most of his opportunity and on any other team should be the starting left fielder going forward, at least against right-handed pitchers (though he actually hit lefties better in a small sample). But on this team, in this season, he'll have to bide his time for another opening.

YEAR	TEAM	LVL	AGE	PA	DRC+	VORP	BABIP	BRR	FRAA	WARP
2017	ABQ	AAA	26	475	125	38.1	.361	2.5	CF(62): 1.3, LF(34): 5.7	3.7
2017	COL	MLB	26	32	64	-1.1	.353	-0.5	RF(3): -0.1, CF(3): -0.3	-0.2
2018	ABQ	AAA	27	471	144	39.6	.345	3.5	CF(65): 4.2, LF(30): 6.1	5.5
2018	COL	MLB	27	37	52	-3.5	.176	0.1	CF(5): -0.1, LF(3): -0.9	-0.2
2019	SWB	AAA	28	114	115	6.7	.308	1.2	CF(15): 0.4, LF(7): 1.4	0.8
2019	NYA	MLB	28	296	112	13.1	.333	2.4	LF(59): 5.3, RF(19): -0.5	1.9
2020	*NYA*	*MLB*	*29*	*245*	*91*	*5.2*	*.283*	*0.3*	*CF 2, RF 0*	*0.9*

Mike Tauchman, continued

Batted Ball Distribution

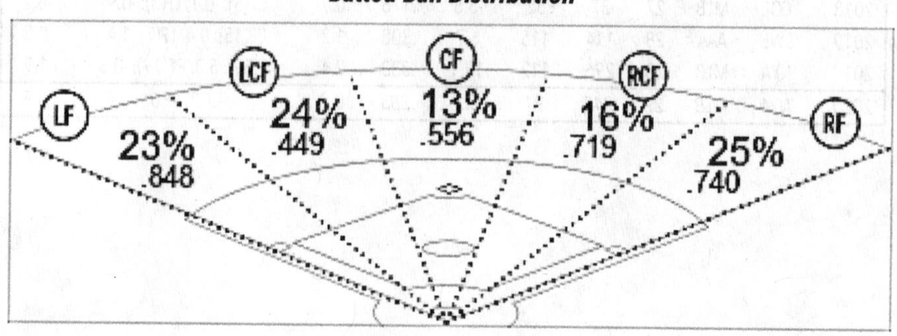

Strike Zone vs LHP **Strike Zone vs RHP**

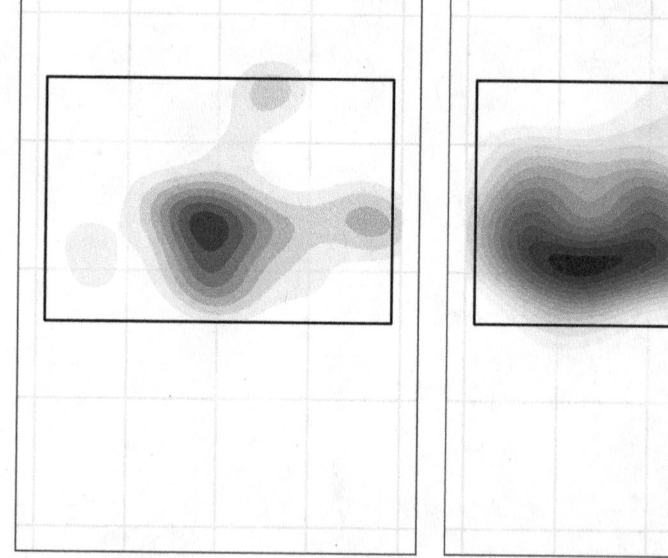

Gleyber Torres MI

Born: 12/13/96 Age: 23 Bats: R Throws: R
Height: 6'1" Weight: 200 Origin: International Free Agent, 2013

YEAR	TEAM	LVL	AGE	PA	R	2B	3B	HR	RBI	BB	K	SB	CS	AVG/OBP/SLG
2017	TRN	AA	20	139	22	10	1	5	18	17	21	5	4	.273/.367/.496
2017	SWB	AAA	20	96	9	4	1	2	16	13	26	2	2	.309/.406/.457
2018	SWB	AAA	21	56	6	3	1	1	11	5	10	1	1	.347/.393/.510
2018	NYA	MLB	21	484	54	16	1	24	77	42	122	6	2	.271/.340/.480
2019	NYA	MLB	22	604	96	26	0	38	90	48	129	5	2	.278/.337/.535
2020	*NYA*	*MLB*	*23*	*595*	*77*	*23*	*2*	*31*	*88*	*49*	*134*	*11*	*6*	*.259/.325/.479*

Comparables: Carlos Correa, Rougned Odor, Rafael Devers

Webster's Dictionary defines a beneficiary owner as "one who enjoys the benefit of a property of which another is the legal owner." Peter Angelos may be the most famous legal owner of the Baltimore Orioles franchise, but Torres established his own control over the organization in 2019. In 18 games against his moribund division foe, the sophomore shortstop hit .394/.467/1.045 with 13 of his team-leading 38 homers, each one slowly destroying the professional brain of Orioles' television announcer Gary Thorne. The 13th and final homer on August 12th—his third of the day, spanning both ends of a doubleheader—caused the MASN broadcaster to just exasperatedly yell "You've got to be kidding me!"

Thorne wasn't the only one to throw that phrase at the budding star. Whether it's the stepped-up power or the ability to play any position on the infield without missing a beat, Torres has become a core tenet of this great Yankees team. And in an effort to be appreciated outside of New York as well, his 1.078 OPS in the 2019 postseason put an exclamation point on his season. The infield will now, and likely for the next decade, be built around Torres playing his natural shortstop. Alongside Aaron Judge, Torres is the future of the franchise.

YEAR	TEAM	LVL	AGE	PA	DRC+	VORP	BABIP	BRR	FRAA	WARP
2017	TRN	AA	20	139	138	15.3	.295	1.3	SS(19): 2.2, 3B(6): 0.8	1.5
2017	SWB	AAA	20	96	127	7.1	.426	-1.8	SS(9): 1.0, 3B(9): 1.8	0.7
2018	SWB	AAA	21	56	119	4.7	.400	0.1	3B(8): 0.6, 2B(3): 0.0	0.4
2018	NYA	MLB	21	484	121	23.9	.321	0.8	2B(109): 5.4, SS(21): 1.5	3.7
2019	NYA	MLB	22	604	124	43.8	.296	-1.0	SS(77): -1.4, 2B(65): -1.0	3.9
2020	*NYA*	*MLB*	*23*	*595*	*111*	*30.4*	*.291*	*-0.8*	*SS 2, 2B 0*	*3.4*

Gleyber Torres, continued

Batted Ball Distribution

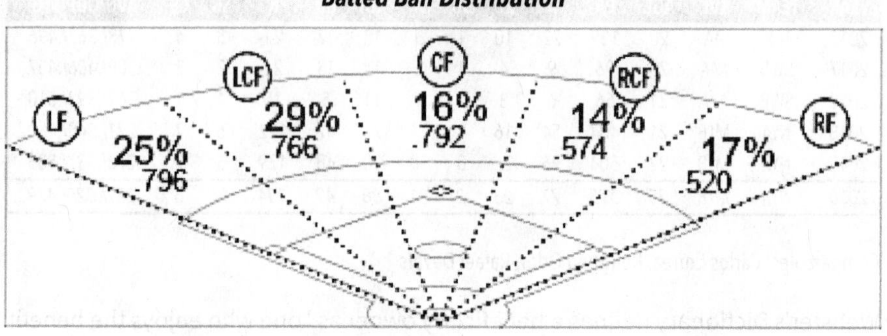

Strike Zone vs LHP

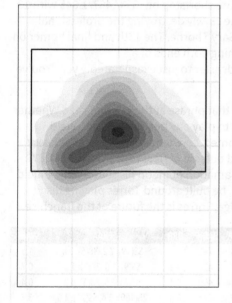

Strike Zone vs RHP

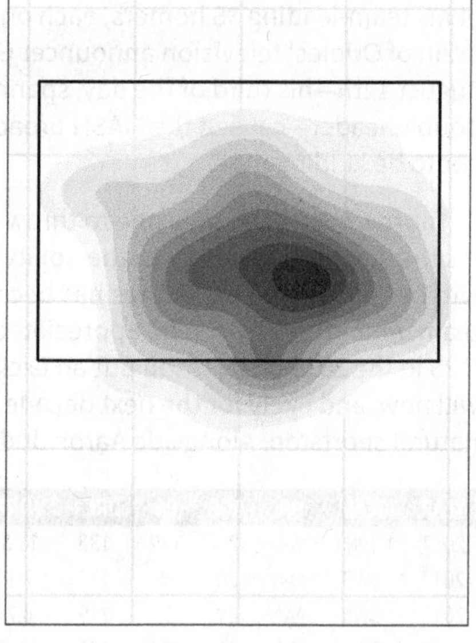

Gio Urshela 3B

Born: 10/11/91 Age: 28 Bats: R Throws: R
Height: 6'0" Weight: 220 Origin: International Free Agent, 2008

YEAR	TEAM	LVL	AGE	PA	R	2B	3B	HR	RBI	BB	K	SB	CS	AVG/OBP/SLG
2017	COH	AAA	25	325	34	12	1	6	34	20	45	0	0	.266/.321/.374
2017	CLE	MLB	25	165	14	7	0	1	15	8	22	0	0	.224/.262/.288
2018	COH	AAA	26	42	6	4	0	0	7	5	9	0	0	.324/.405/.432
2018	BUF	AAA	26	91	7	3	0	0	5	4	9	0	0	.244/.275/.279
2018	SWB	AAA	26	107	14	7	2	2	12	4	13	0	0	.307/.340/.475
2018	TOR	MLB	26	46	7	1	0	1	3	2	10	0	0	.233/.283/.326
2019	NYA	MLB	27	476	73	34	0	21	74	25	87	1	1	.314/.355/.534
2020	*NYA*	*MLB*	*28*	*455*	*49*	*23*	*1*	*16*	*57*	*24*	*89*	*1*	*0*	*.265/.309/.435*

Comparables: Danny Valencia, Leury García, Donovan Solano

It may not have been a bastion of stardom, but Urshela was quite the unlikely candidate to finish the decade with the highest single-season OPS of any Yankee third baseman. After all, he came into the 2019 season with a career .589 mark and a minor-league assignment. In his age-27 season, everything changed. Urshela had a full-on breakout, filling the hole left by Miguel Andújar with ease and likely stealing the starting spot for good. His defense has always been top notch, flashy and highlight reel worthy, but desperately waiting for his bat to catch up. Well, it's here. The juiced balls certainly played a factor in the power jump, but to go from a hitter who had never broken .300 in the minors, aside from two small-sample Triple-A appearances, to the fifth-best batting average in the American League is a substantial improvement. With a newfound aggressiveness at the plate, and a distinct defensive advantage over his competition, Urshela has the all-around skill to man the position well into the next decade.

YEAR	TEAM	LVL	AGE	PA	DRC+	VORP	BABIP	BRR	FRAA	WARP
2017	COH	AAA	25	325	97	1.3	.294	-3.5	3B(60): 0.3, SS(16): 1.0	0.8
2017	CLE	MLB	25	165	79	-5.8	.256	-0.5	3B(60): 0.9, SS(5): -0.1	0.2
2018	COH	AAA	26	42	101	3.1	.429	0.3	2B(4): 0.3, 3B(4): 0.3	0.2
2018	BUF	AAA	26	91	105	-3.4	.269	-0.1	3B(14): -1.4, 1B(7): 0.2	0.3
2018	SWB	AAA	26	107	104	5.2	.337	0.0	3B(20): 1.1, SS(8): -1.0	0.5
2018	TOR	MLB	26	46	82	-1.4	.281	-0.2	3B(10): -0.8, SS(8): -0.3	-0.1
2019	NYA	MLB	27	476	121	31.2	.349	-1.8	3B(123): 5.8, LF(1): 0.0	3.4
2020	*NYA*	*MLB*	*28*	*455*	*98*	*8.5*	*.301*	*-1.0*	*3B 2*	*1.1*

Gio Urshela, continued

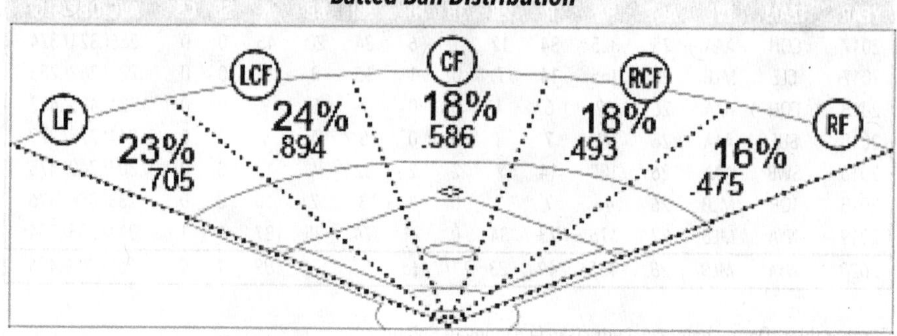

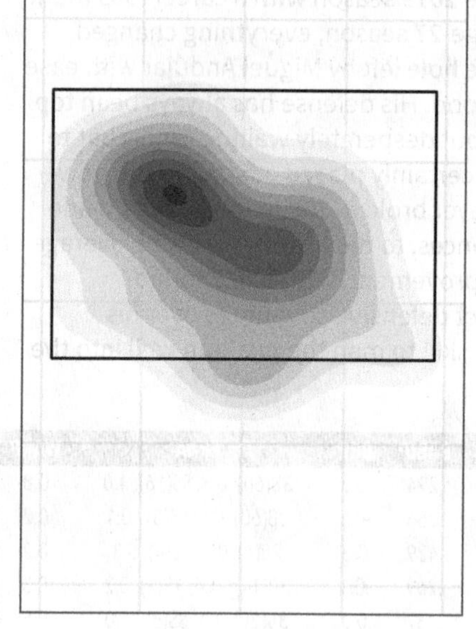

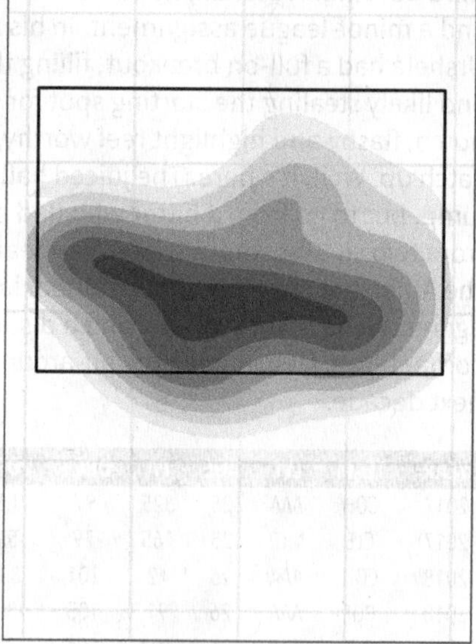

Luke Voit 1B

Born: 02/13/91 Age: 29 Bats: R Throws: R
Height: 6'3" Weight: 225 Origin: Round 22, 2013 Draft (#665 overall)

YEAR	TEAM	LVL	AGE	PA	R	2B	3B	HR	RBI	BB	K	SB	CS	AVG/OBP/SLG
2017	MEM	AAA	26	307	35	23	1	13	50	29	53	1	1	.327/.407/.565
2017	SLN	MLB	26	124	18	9	0	4	18	7	31	0	0	.246/.306/.430
2018	MEM	AAA	27	271	35	16	2	9	36	31	49	0	1	.299/.391/.500
2018	SWB	AAA	27	32	2	2	0	1	3	3	7	0	0	.310/.375/.483
2018	SLN	MLB	27	13	2	0	0	1	3	2	4	0	0	.182/.308/.455
2018	NYA	MLB	27	148	28	5	0	14	33	15	39	0	0	.333/.405/.689
2019	NYA	MLB	28	510	72	21	1	21	62	71	142	0	0	.263/.378/.464
2020	*NYA*	*MLB*	*29*	*560*	*75*	*22*	*2*	*28*	*83*	*62*	*156*	*1*	*0*	*.264/.356/.486*

Comparables: Tyler White, Justin Bour, Craig Wilson

Frankie Valli voice
You're not too good to be true
Can't take my eyes off of you.
Oh God, I think you're so clutch
I wanna hold you so much.

Was Luke a fluke? Not at all. With a delicate skip and a jump, Voit's plus power and infectious energy complemented the Bronx Bomber line up perfectly. Questions about whether or not he could play up to the standards he set in his abbreviated torching of the American League down the stretch in 2018 lingered throughout the offseason, but he played a huge role in carrying the team through a first half marred by injury. His overall numbers were soured by an abdominal injury that turned into a sports hernia and required offseason surgery, as he was hitting .280/.393/.503 when it struck and .228/.348/.368 afterwards. Once he's back 100 percent health wise? Oh, what a night.

YEAR	TEAM	LVL	AGE	PA	DRC+	VORP	BABIP	BRR	FRAA	WARP
2017	MEM	AAA	26	307	155	29.6	.368	-3.6	1B(62): 4.3	2.6
2017	SLN	MLB	26	124	88	0.8	.304	-0.3	1B(31): 1.6	0.2
2018	MEM	AAA	27	271	133	17.0	.345	-1.3	1B(56): 2.1, LF(1): -0.1	1.5
2018	SWB	AAA	27	32	114	1.3	.381	-0.1	1B(3): 0.2	0.1
2018	SLN	MLB	27	13	159	1.4	.167	0.1	1B(3): 0.3	0.2
2018	NYA	MLB	27	148	155	18.2	.380	1.1	1B(32): -2.7	1.1
2019	NYA	MLB	28	510	118	20.1	.345	-3.2	1B(83): -3.2	1.3
2020	*NYA*	*MLB*	*29*	*560*	*125*	*27.4*	*.332*	*-1.1*	*1B 1*	*2.9*

Luke Voit, continued

Batted Ball Distribution

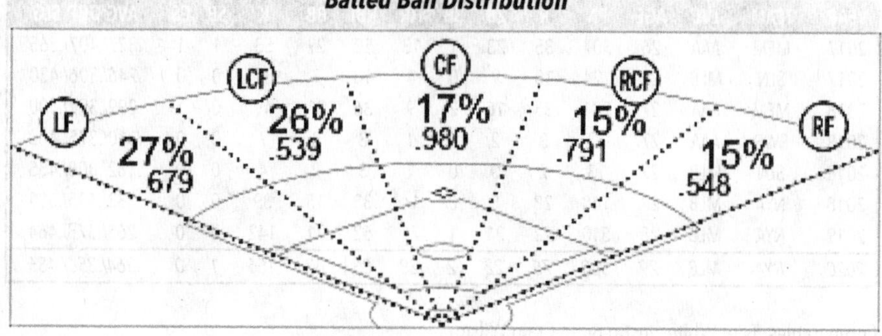

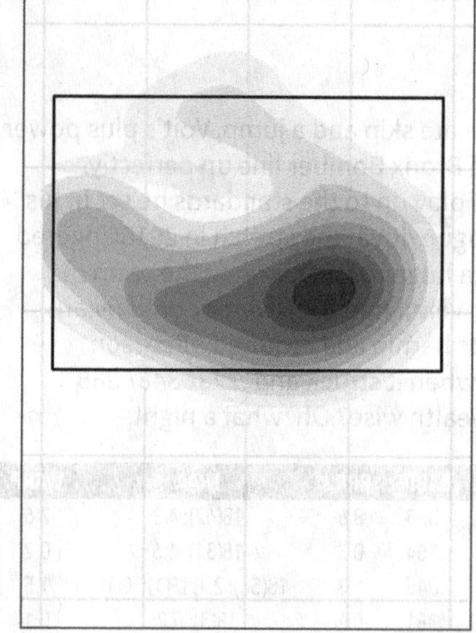

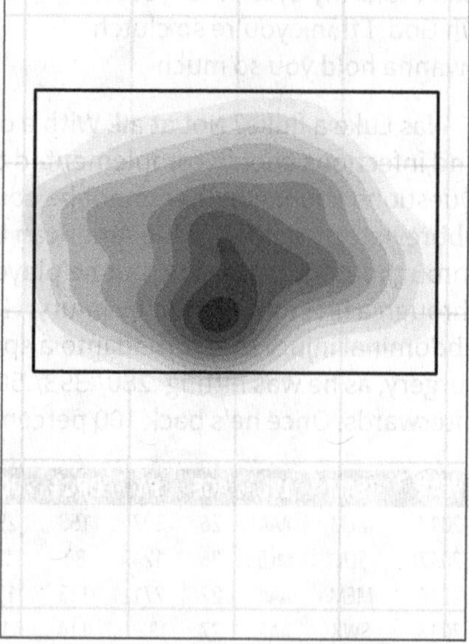

Tyler Wade INF

Born: 11/23/94 Age: 25 Bats: L Throws: R
Height: 6'1" Weight: 185 Origin: Round 4, 2013 Draft (#134 overall)

YEAR	TEAM	LVL	AGE	PA	R	2B	3B	HR	RBI	BB	K	SB	CS	AVG/OBP/SLG
2017	SWB	AAA	22	388	68	22	4	7	31	38	75	26	5	.310/.382/.460
2017	NYA	MLB	22	63	7	4	0	0	2	5	19	1	1	.155/.222/.224
2018	SWB	AAA	23	408	46	18	4	4	27	37	82	11	8	.255/.328/.360
2018	NYA	MLB	23	70	8	4	0	1	5	4	23	1	0	.167/.214/.273
2019	SWB	AAA	24	335	51	19	4	4	38	23	76	13	5	.296/.352/.425
2019	NYA	MLB	24	108	16	3	1	2	11	11	28	7	0	.245/.330/.362
2020	*NYA*	*MLB*	*25*	*175*	*16*	*7*	*1*	*3*	*16*	*13*	*49*	*5*	*2*	*.226/.290/.334*

Comparables: Jerry Snyder, Jonathan Villar, Tim Beckham

Wade experienced a bit of a rollercoaster throughout the season, from thinking he had earned a spot on the Opening Day roster only to be left off in the final hour to spending more time traveling to and from Scranton than on the playing field. His versatility came in handy as the natural infielder racked up innings at all three outfield positions, second, third and shortstop. Speed on the basepaths remains his strongest tool. While he often looks outmatched at the plate, he's a constant threat to steal once he reaches base and scoring from first is never off the table. He's in Quad-A limbo, but makes a good case for himself as a bench player. He's the perfect pinch runner or late inning defensive replacement, though a second-division team would be happy enough to play him every day.

YEAR	TEAM	LVL	AGE	PA	DRC+	VORP	BABIP	BRR	FRAA	WARP
2017	SWB	AAA	22	388	130	30.4	.375	3.0	SS(54): -2.3, 2B(13): 2.8	3.4
2017	NYA	MLB	22	63	65	-3.3	.231	0.7	2B(15): -0.8, SS(7): 0.0	-0.1
2018	SWB	AAA	23	408	97	8.5	.318	-2.1	SS(51): -0.2, LF(12): 2.1	1.7
2018	NYA	MLB	23	70	55	-2.9	.238	1.7	2B(26): -0.6, RF(5): -0.1	-0.1
2019	SWB	AAA	24	335	92	13.8	.381	1.6	SS(43): 2.6, 2B(28): 0.7	1.4
2019	NYA	MLB	24	108	73	-0.3	.328	0.5	2B(18): 1.8, LF(14): 0.1	0.1
2020	*NYA*	*MLB*	*25*	*175*	*69*	*0.2*	*.306*	*0.6*	*SS 0, 2B 2*	*0.2*

Tyler Wade, continued

Batted Ball Distribution

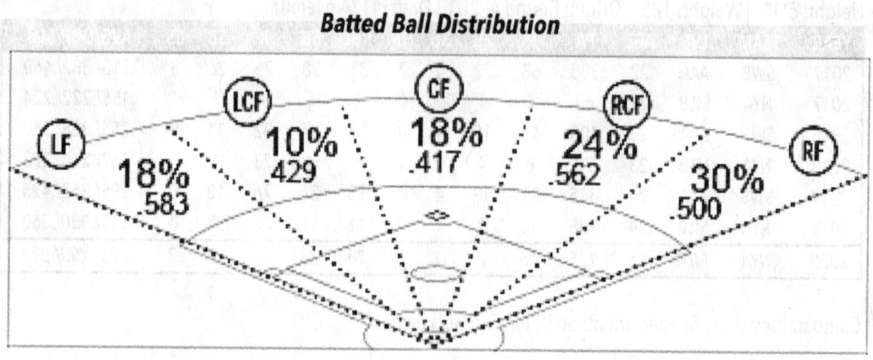

Strike Zone vs LHP

Strike Zone vs RHP

Luis Avilán LHP

Born: 07/19/89 Age: 30 Bats: L Throws: L
Height: 6'2" Weight: 220 Origin: International Free Agent, 2005

YEAR	TEAM	LVL	AGE	W	L	SV	G	GS	IP	H	HR	BB/9	K/9	K	GB%	BABIP
2017	LAN	MLB	27	2	3	0	61	0	46	42	2	4.3	10.2	52	56%	.342
2018	CHA	MLB	28	2	1	2	58	0	39²	40	2	3.2	10.4	46	37%	.352
2018	PHI	MLB	28	0	0	0	12	0	5²	4	1	6.4	7.9	5	38%	.200
2019	NYN	MLB	29	4	0	0	45	0	32	33	5	3.9	8.4	30	45%	.315
2020	*NYN*	*MLB*	*30*	*2*	*2*	*0*	*33*	*0*	*35*	*30*	*5*	*3.9*	*8.9*	*35*	*45%*	*.276*

Comparables: Eric O'Flaherty, Neftalí Feliz, Robbie Ross Jr.

Avilán's overall numbers don't look pretty for the year, but he more than accomplished what was tasked of him when the Mets penned him to a modest one-year deal last offseason. After all, lefties hit just .102/.185/.184 off him. Yet 62 percent of the batters he faced during 2019 were right-handed, which was highly questionable decision making by Mickey Callaway given that Avilán's OPS when hitters were allowed the platoon advantage was nearly 700 points higher than without. Yes, that's not a typo. Seven hundred. The new rule changes are not going to be his friend.

YEAR	TEAM	LVL	AGE	WHIP	ERA	DRA	WARP	MPH	FB%	WHF	CSP
2017	LAN	MLB	27	1.39	2.93	3.33	0.9	94.6	41.7	15.1	33
2018	CHA	MLB	28	1.36	3.86	4.83	0.0	92.9	35.5	10.8	42.3
2018	PHI	MLB	28	1.41	3.18	5.26	0.0	92.3	41.8	13.3	43.6
2019	NYN	MLB	29	1.47	5.06	5.10	0.1	91.9	29.5	11.7	37.7
2020	*NYN*	*MLB*	*30*	*1.29*	*3.87*	*3.95*	*0.6*	*92.3*	*35.3*	*12.4*	*38*

Luis Avilán, continued

Pitch Shape vs LHH

Pitch Shape vs RHH

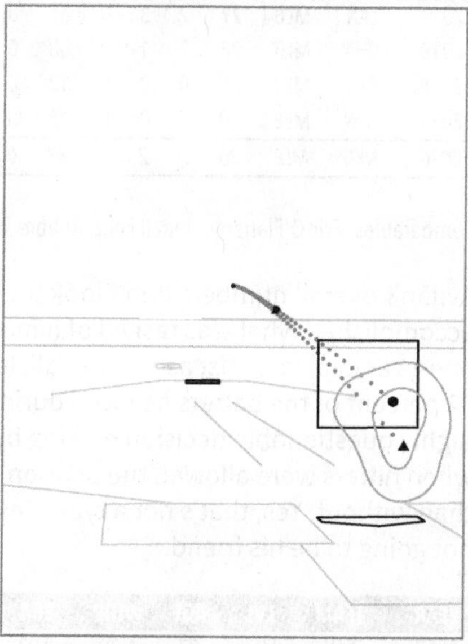

Type	Frequency	Velocity	H Movement	V Movement
● Fastball	29.5%	90.6 [95]	13.9 [69]	-20.2 [89]
□ Sinker				
+ Cutter				
▲ Changeup	58.3%	82.6 [91]	12.6 [93]	-30.2 [92]
✕ Splitter				
▽ Slider				
◇ Curveball	12.2%	75.4 [90]	-8.5 [104]	-48.6 [98]
⊕ Slow Curveball				
✱ Knuckleball				
▼ Screwball				

Chad Bettis RHP

Born: 04/26/89 Age: 31 Bats: R Throws: R

Height: 6'0" Weight: 201 Origin: Round 2, 2010 Draft (#76 overall)

YEAR	TEAM	LVL	AGE	W	L	SV	G	GS	IP	H	HR	BB/9	K/9	K	GB%	BABIP
2017	ABQ	AAA	28	0	3	0	4	4	18^2	22	2	2.9	5.3	11	55%	.312
2017	COL	MLB	28	2	4	0	9	9	46^1	52	8	2.1	5.8	30	50%	.293
2018	ABQ	AAA	29	0	0	0	3	3	14	16	2	1.9	6.4	10	51%	.311
2018	COL	MLB	29	5	2	0	27	20	120^1	121	18	3.5	6.0	80	51%	.280
2019	COL	MLB	30	1	6	1	39	3	63^2	78	10	3.0	5.9	42	61%	.325
2020	*COL*	*MLB*	*31*	*2*	*2*	*0*	*33*	*0*	*35*	*39*	*5*	*3.2*	*7.0*	*27*	*57%*	*.314*

Comparables: Joe Kelly, Wily Peralta, Jeff Manship

After three starts, Bettis had allowed 13 runs in the same number of innings. He didn't get to make any more in 2019. Moving to relief can often bring a clear velocity bump, and Reliever Bettis was no exception: he gained almost two full ticks on his fastball on average and nearly three by mid-season. What he failed to gain was strikeouts. A brief whiff surge in May gave way to a worse strikeout rate than Starter Bettis', as the 30-year-old punched out just 17 of the 139 batters he faced from the start of June onwards. The impingements that ended his season and led to surgery on both hips may have had something to do with that.

YEAR	TEAM	LVL	AGE	WHIP	ERA	DRA	WARP	MPH	FB%	WHF	CSP
2017	ABQ	AAA	28	1.50	4.82	5.17	0.1				
2017	COL	MLB	28	1.36	5.05	4.39	0.6	92.9	51.9	9.7	43
2018	ABQ	AAA	29	1.36	5.14	4.37	0.2				
2018	COL	MLB	29	1.40	5.01	5.74	-0.6	93.5	41.4	9.2	46.9
2019	COL	MLB	30	1.55	6.08	5.22	0.2	95.6	39.1	9.7	49.1
2020	*COL*	*MLB*	*31*	*1.48*	*5.05*	*5.13*	*0.1*	*93.3*	*41.9*	*9.4*	*46.6*

Chad Bettis, continued

Pitch Shape vs LHH | **Pitch Shape vs RHH**

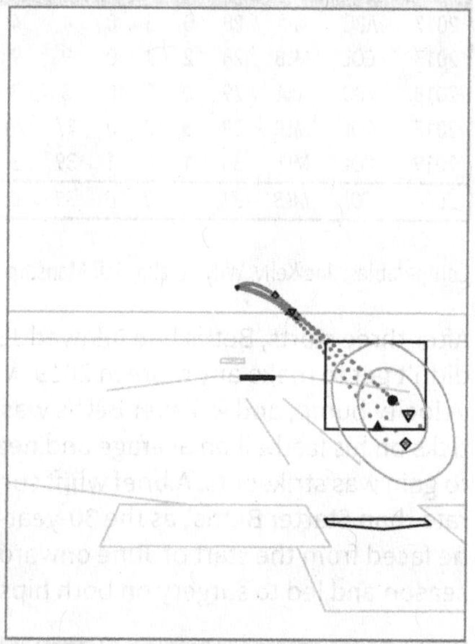

Type	Frequency	Velocity	H Movement	V Movement
● Fastball	38.1%	93.2 [102]	-5.2 [107]	-16.7 [98]
□ Sinker				
+ Cutter				
▲ Changeup	31.5%	87.2 [107]	-7.6 [117]	-27.9 [99]
✕ Splitter				
▽ Slider	17.4%	88.9 [119]	3.8 [95]	-25.5 [122]
◇ Curveball	12.0%	77.5 [96]	10.7 [113]	-48 [99]
⊕ Slow Curveball				
✱ Knuckleball				
▼ Screwball				

Zack Britton LHP

Born: 12/22/87 Age: 32 Bats: L Throws: L
Height: 6'3" Weight: 195 Origin: Round 3, 2006 Draft (#85 overall)

YEAR	TEAM	LVL	AGE	W	L	SV	G	GS	IP	H	HR	BB/9	K/9	K	GB%	BABIP
2017	BAL	MLB	29	2	1	15	38	0	37^1	39	1	4.3	7.0	29	75%	.336
2018	BAL	MLB	30	1	0	4	16	0	15^2	11	1	5.7	7.5	13	64%	.263
2018	NYA	MLB	30	1	0	3	25	0	25	18	2	4.0	7.6	21	78%	.229
2019	NYA	MLB	31	3	1	3	66	0	61^1	38	3	4.7	7.8	53	77%	.224
2020	*NYA*	*MLB*	*32*	*3*	*3*	*5*	*56*	*0*	*60*	*47*	*5*	*4.1*	*9.2*	*61*	*74%*	*.272*

Comparables: Brett Cecil, Brian Matusz, Eric O'Flaherty

In another world, Britton would be the Yankees closer. In many worlds, he should be. He was the team's most consistent reliever, turning in another extremely strong year, both in the regular season and playoffs—his highest ERA in an individual month was 3.60. Speaking of consistency, in a surprise to absolutely no one, Britton had the highest ground-ball rate among relievers at 77 percent, combating the juiced ball with ease. One of the Yankees' Four Horsemen of the Apocalypse, Britton's trot from the bullpen invoked fear in his opponents, his sinker's as deadly as ever and it shows no real signs of stopping.

YEAR	TEAM	LVL	AGE	WHIP	ERA	DRA	WARP	MPH	FB%	WHF	CSP
2017	BAL	MLB	29	1.53	2.89	5.91	-0.3	97.6	94.7	12.4	42.2
2018	BAL	MLB	30	1.34	3.45	7.71	-0.5	96.6	94.4	14.5	42.3
2018	NYA	MLB	30	1.16	2.88	6.55	-0.5	96.7	93.1	12.3	42.8
2019	NYA	MLB	31	1.14	1.91	3.47	1.2	96.3	86.4	11.5	42.5
2020	*NYA*	*MLB*	*32*	*1.24*	*2.90*	*3.27*	*1.2*	*95.7*	*89.3*	*12.1*	*42.1*

Zack Britton, continued

Pitch Shape vs LHH

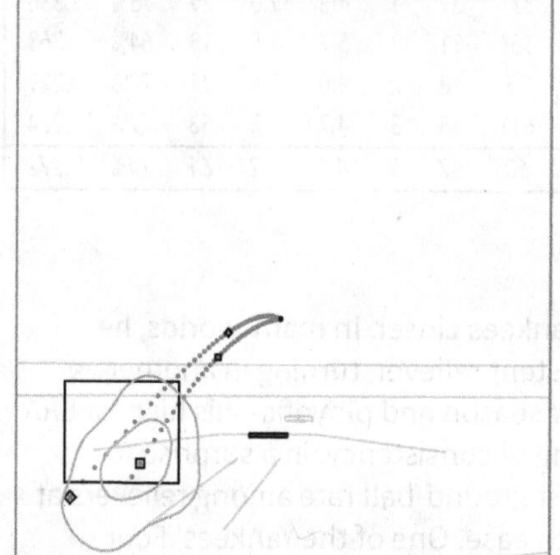

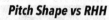

Pitch Shape vs RHH

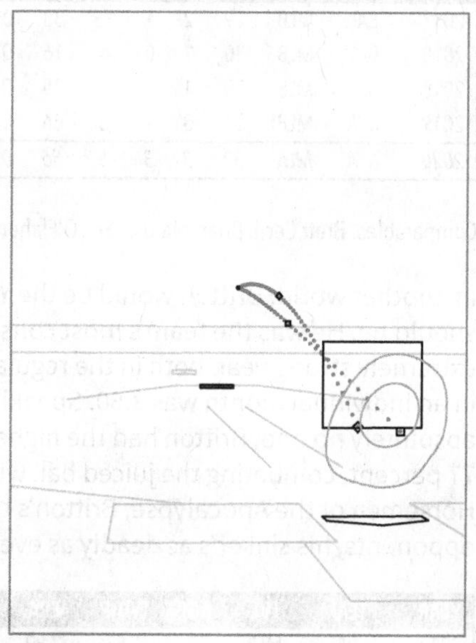

Type	Frequency	Velocity	H Movement	V Movement
● Fastball				
□ Sinker	86.4%	94.9 [112]	11.3 [109]	-20.8 [99]
+ Cutter				
▲ Changeup				
✕ Splitter				
▽ Slider				
◇ Curveball	13.6%	80.7 [107]	-9.6 [109]	-44.4 [107]
⊕ Slow Curveball				
✱ Knuckleball				
▼ Screwball				

Luis Cessa RHP

Born: 04/25/92 Age: 28 Bats: R Throws: R
Height: 6'0" Weight: 210 Origin: International Free Agent, 2008

YEAR	TEAM	LVL	AGE	W	L	SV	G	GS	IP	H	HR	BB/9	K/9	K	GB%	BABIP
2017	SWB	AAA	25	4	6	0	14	13	78^{1}	75	7	3.0	7.7	67	48%	.304
2017	NYA	MLB	25	0	3	0	10	5	36	36	7	4.2	7.5	30	46%	.282
2018	TRN	AA	26	0	1	0	2	2	10	6	0	0.9	10.8	12	50%	.250
2018	SWB	AAA	26	3	0	0	6	5	26^{1}	19	1	1.4	8.5	25	40%	.250
2018	NYA	MLB	26	1	4	2	16	5	44^{2}	51	5	2.6	7.9	39	48%	.333
2019	NYA	MLB	27	2	1	1	43	0	81	75	14	3.4	8.3	75	48%	.282
2020	*NYA*	*MLB*	*28*	*3*	*3*	*0*	*51*	*0*	*54*	*52*	*9*	*3.2*	*8.7*	*52*	*47%*	*.291*

Comparables: Héctor Noesi, Jake Buchanan, Jakob Junis

Patience is a virtue. Brian Cashman stuck with Cessa when the whole world was screaming for him to be DFA'd and he quietly put together a solid year. In the new age of the bullpen, Cessa has real value—he eats innings and can bridge the gap between starters and elite bullpen arms, all while keeping the game within reach. His slider is easily his best offering and he relied on it heavily this season, throwing the pitch more than 50 percent of the time. His most notable performance came in the ALCS, where he pitched a pair of scoreless innings in each of his appearances. In a bullpen with much bigger names, Cessa has finally figured it out and turned himself into a trusted arm.

YEAR	TEAM	LVL	AGE	WHIP	ERA	DRA	WARP	MPH	FB%	WHF	CSP
2017	SWB	AAA	25	1.29	3.45	4.57	1.0				
2017	NYA	MLB	25	1.47	4.75	4.72	0.3	97.7	41.8	11.5	44.5
2018	TRN	AA	26	0.70	2.70	2.96	0.3				
2018	SWB	AAA	26	0.87	2.73	2.52	0.9				
2018	NYA	MLB	26	1.43	5.24	3.23	1.0	97.1	41.6	12.6	45.7
2019	NYA	MLB	27	1.31	4.11	4.82	0.5	96.5	41.9	13.8	44
2020	*NYA*	*MLB*	*28*	*1.32*	*4.19*	*4.51*	*0.4*	*96.3*	*42.1*	*13.2*	*45*

Luis Cessa, continued

Pitch Shape vs LHH

Pitch Shape vs RHH

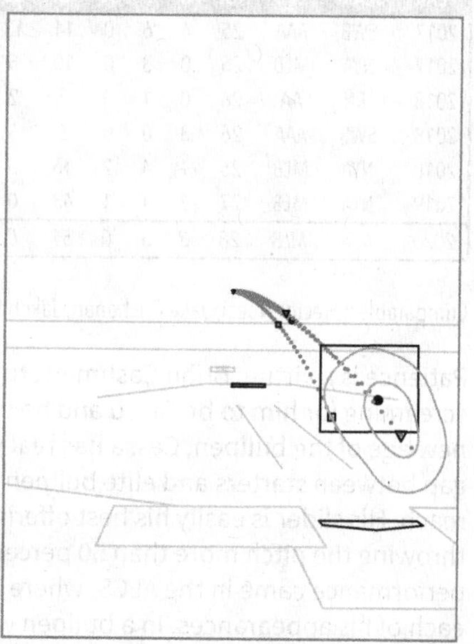

Type	Frequency	Velocity	H Movement	V Movement
● Fastball	34.0%	94.7 [107]	-7.9 [95]	-13.4 [107]
□ Sinker	7.9%	93.8 [106]	-12.9 [98]	-17.2 [111]
+ Cutter				
▲ Changeup	7.2%	87.1 [107]	-10.6 [103]	-25 [107]
✕ Splitter				
▽ Slider	49.9%	84.9 [102]	0.9 [83]	-33.2 [100]
◇ Curveball				
⊕ Slow Curveball				
✱ Knuckleball				
▼ Screwball				

Aroldis Chapman LHP

Born: 02/28/88 Age: 32 Bats: L Throws: L
Height: 6'4" Weight: 212 Origin: International Free Agent, 2010

YEAR	TEAM	LVL	AGE	W	L	SV	G	GS	IP	H	HR	BB/9	K/9	K	GB%	BABIP
2017	NYA	MLB	29	4	3	22	52	0	50^{1}	37	3	3.6	12.3	69	48%	.298
2018	NYA	MLB	30	3	0	32	55	0	51^{1}	24	2	5.3	16.3	93	46%	.268
2019	NYA	MLB	31	3	2	37	60	0	57	38	3	3.9	13.4	85	42%	.292
2020	*NYA*	*MLB*	*32*	*3*	*3*	*46*	*56*	*0*	*60*	*40*	*6*	*4.1*	*14.1*	*93*	*43%*	*.291*

Comparables: Craig Kimbrel, Kenley Jansen, Dellin Betances

Chapman's still a fireballer, despite a consistent, albeit minor, dip in velocity the last few seasons. The subtle decline is a blessing in disguise, causing Chapman to utilize his slider more often—the mix making both pitches more effective. Fewer strikeouts and stare downs, but more outs and still the same amount of sweat and turtlenecks. He's an elite closer and even if he no longer tops the velocity leaderboards, he has the formula to repeat this season's success as he ages. Clearly the Yankees agree as Chapman was able to leverage the opt-out clause in his contract to get an extra year and $18 million from the team; extending his stay in New York at least through the end of the 2022 season.

YEAR	TEAM	LVL	AGE	WHIP	ERA	DRA	WARP	MPH	FB%	WHF	CSP
2017	NYA	MLB	29	1.13	3.22	3.50	0.9	102.5	76.8	15.2	48.5
2018	NYA	MLB	30	1.05	2.45	2.13	1.7	102.4	73.8	16.8	45.8
2019	NYA	MLB	31	1.11	2.21	2.57	1.7	101.5	68.8	14.9	49.2
2020	*NYA*	*MLB*	*32*	*1.12*	*2.51*	*2.90*	*1.5*	*101.0*	*71.6*	*15.4*	*47.5*

Aroldis Chapman, continued

Pitch Shape vs LHH

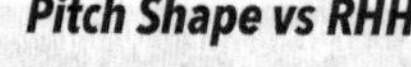

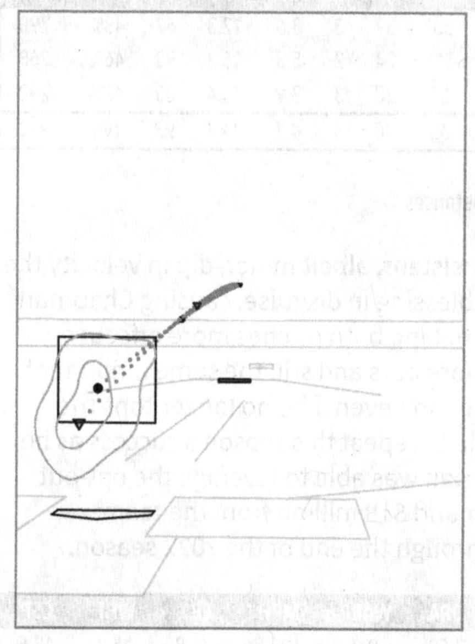

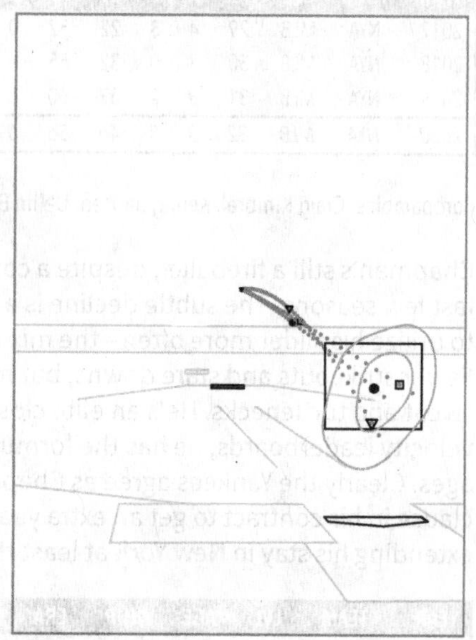

Type	Frequency	Velocity	H Movement	V Movement
● Fastball	58.8%	98.3 [117]	3.3 [116]	-9.1 [118]
□ Sinker	9.9%	100.5 [141]	11.1 [110]	-10.5 [135]
+ Cutter				
▲ Changeup				
✕ Splitter				
▽ Slider	31.1%	85.5 [104]	-9.5 [119]	-32.8 [101]
◇ Curveball				
⊕ Slow Curveball				
✱ Knuckleball				
▼ Screwball				

Gerrit Cole RHP

Born: 09/08/90 Age: 29 Bats: R Throws: R
Height: 6'4" Weight: 225 Origin: Round 1, 2011 Draft (#1 overall)

YEAR	TEAM	LVL	AGE	W	L	SV	G	GS	IP	H	HR	BB/9	K/9	K	GB%	BABIP
2017	PIT	MLB	26	12	12	0	33	33	203	199	31	2.4	8.7	196	47%	.298
2018	HOU	MLB	27	15	5	0	32	32	200[1]	143	19	2.9	12.4	276	38%	.286
2019	HOU	MLB	28	20	5	0	33	33	212[1]	142	29	2.0	13.8	326	41%	.275
2020	*NYA*	*MLB*	*29*	*16*	*6*	*0*	*31*	*31*	*200*	*152*	*24*	*2.7*	*13.6*	*255*	*41%*	*.309*

Comparables: Roger Clemens, Josh Johnson, Tommy Hanson

To give you a sense of just how dominant Cole was down the stretch in 2019, here is a stat for you: he was 5-5 with a 4.02 ERA at the end of May, then he finished second in the AL Cy Young race. In his final 21 starts, he had a 1.73 ERA, allowing 30 walks and 27 earned runs over 140 2/3 innings while striking out 214. Two hundred fourteen! It was like he turned the calendar to June and had the thought, "Hey why don't I try to just humiliate every single person that comes into the batter's box?" and it worked. He set a major-league record by striking out double-digit batters in nine straight appearances to end the season. Then he went and did it in his first two postseason appearances. He set a new record for a single season K/9.

He throws upper-90s heat with ease, and much like the guy he lost the Cy Young to, teammate Justin Verlander, he saves an extra gear for when he needs it most. His slider doesn't so much fall off the table as it breaks the table in half and then laughs at you for putting a silly table in its way. When he gets bored and wants to play around, he'll throw an 88 mph change up to lefties and when he really feels like slowing it down he'll casually toss in an 82 mph curveball. He's unhittable. He's not even 30. He's going to make the Yankees very happy for a long time. And all it took was money.

YEAR	TEAM	LVL	AGE	WHIP	ERA	DRA	WARP	MPH	FB%	WHF	CSP
2017	PIT	MLB	26	1.25	4.26	3.84	3.9	98.4	60	10.1	49.5
2018	HOU	MLB	27	1.03	2.88	2.55	6.4	99.0	56.3	15.3	49.8
2019	HOU	MLB	28	0.89	2.50	2.36	7.9	99.4	54	18.5	48.8
2020	*NYA*	*MLB*	*29*	*1.06*	*2.52*	*2.99*	*5.7*	*98.3*	*56.3*	*15.4*	*49.3*

Gerrit Cole, continued

Pitch Shape vs LHH

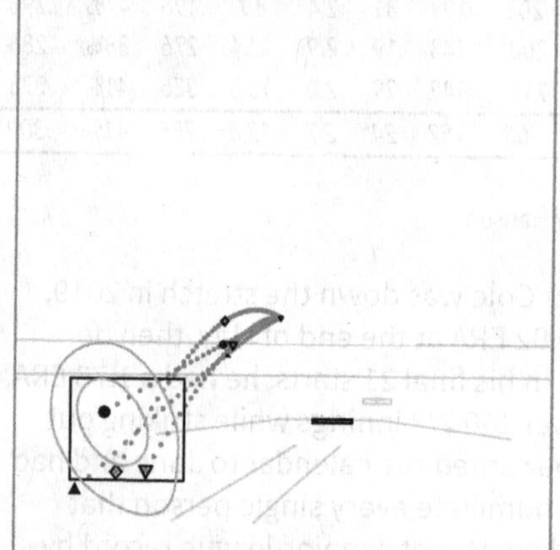

Pitch Shape vs RHH

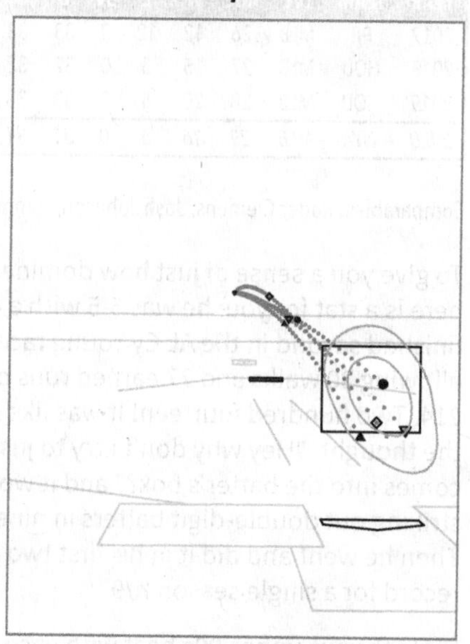

Type	Frequency	Velocity	H Movement	V Movement
● Fastball	53.6%	97.4 [114]	-10 [86]	-10 [115]
□ Sinker				
+ Cutter				
▲ Changeup	7.4%	88.9 [113]	-13.4 [90]	-20.9 [119]
× Splitter				
▽ Slider	23.2%	89.4 [121]	4.6 [98]	-27.9 [115]
◇ Curveball	15.5%	82.8 [114]	10.6 [113]	-49 [97]
⊕ Slow Curveball				
✱ Knuckleball				
▼ Screwball				

Domingo Germán RHP

Born: 08/04/92 Age: 27 Bats: R Throws: R
Height: 6'2" Weight: 175 Origin: International Free Agent, 2009

YEAR	TEAM	LVL	AGE	W	L	SV	G	GS	IP	H	HR	BB/9	K/9	K	GB%	BABIP
2017	TRN	AA	24	1	4	0	6	6	33	32	4	2.7	10.4	38	50%	.318
2017	SWB	AAA	24	7	2	0	14	13	76[1]	59	5	2.6	9.6	81	46%	.274
2017	NYA	MLB	24	0	1	0	7	0	14[1]	11	1	5.7	11.3	18	54%	.294
2018	TAM	A+	25	0	0	0	2	2	6	3	0	3.0	12.0	8	23%	.231
2018	NYA	MLB	25	2	6	0	21	14	85[2]	81	15	3.5	10.7	102	39%	.300
2019	NYA	MLB	26	18	4	0	27	24	143	125	30	2.5	9.6	153	38%	.259
2020	*NYA*	*MLB*	*27*	*4*	*3*	*0*	*34*	*8*	*68*	*59*	*11*	*3.0*	*10.0*	*75*	*38%*	*.280*

Comparables: Mike Clevinger, Brock Stewart, Alec Mills

Germán was placed on administrative leave under the MLB-MLBPA Joint Domestic Violence Policy on September 19, and will miss the first 63 games of the 2020 season as part of an 81-game suspension handed down by Major League Baseball. The National Coalition Against Domestic Violence reports that more than 10 million people a year are physically abused by an intimate partner, and that 1-in-4 women and 1-in-7 men have been victims of severe physical violence by an intimate partner. Even if you don't know it, survivors are all around you. It is far bigger than baseball. Please consider donating to a local women's shelter or charity. If you need help, the 24-hour National Domestic Violence Hotline can be reached at 800-799-7233.

YEAR	TEAM	LVL	AGE	WHIP	ERA	DRA	WARP	MPH	FB%	WHF	CSP
2017	TRN	AA	24	1.27	3.00	4.74	0.2				
2017	SWB	AAA	24	1.06	2.83	2.79	2.4				
2017	NYA	MLB	24	1.40	3.14	3.15	0.3	98.5	50.4	12.7	40
2018	TAM	A+	25	0.83	0.00	2.54	0.2				
2018	NYA	MLB	25	1.33	5.57	4.36	0.9	96.7	46.9	15.5	46.9
2019	NYA	MLB	26	1.15	4.03	4.27	2.3	95.8	44.9	13.9	47.3
2020	*NYA*	*MLB*	*27*	*1.20*	*3.74*	*4.16*	*0.9*	*95.7*	*46.3*	*14.6*	*45.9*

Domingo Germán, continued

Pitch Shape vs LHH

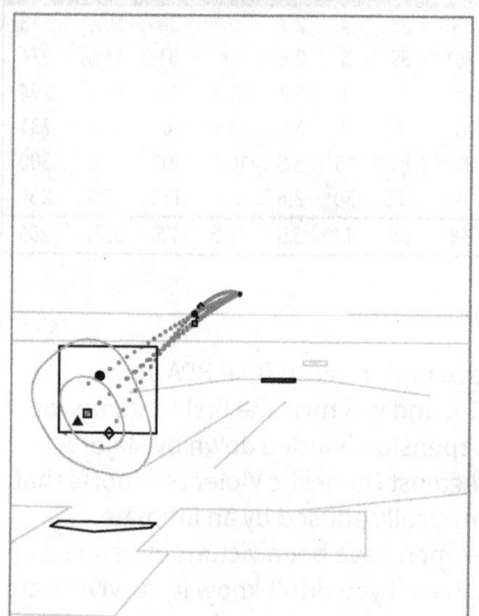

Pitch Shape vs RHH

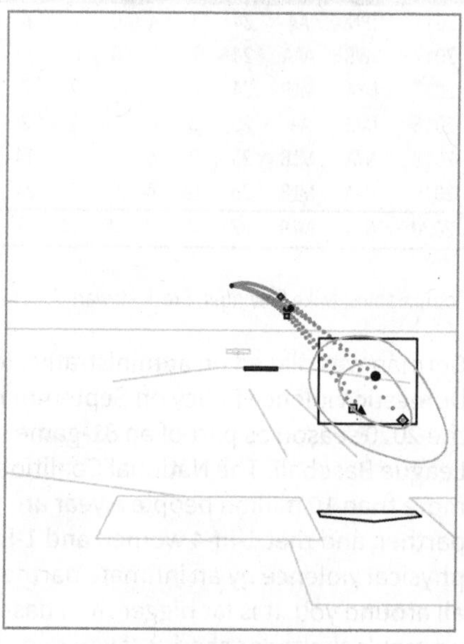

Type	Frequency	Velocity	H Movement	V Movement
● Fastball	33.8%	93.6 [103]	-8.9 [91]	-14.4 [104]
□ Sinker	11.1%	94.2 [108]	-15.2 [84]	-19.8 [102]
+ Cutter				
▲ Changeup	18.9%	87.3 [107]	-15.3 [81]	-23.7 [111]
✕ Splitter				
▽ Slider				
◇ Curveball	34.3%	81.8 [111]	1.4 [75]	-40.4 [115]
⊕ Slow Curveball				
✱ Knuckleball				
▼ Screwball				

Chad Green RHP

Born: 05/24/91 Age: 29 Bats: L Throws: R
Height: 6'3" Weight: 210 Origin: Round 11, 2013 Draft (#336 overall)

YEAR	TEAM	LVL	AGE	W	L	SV	G	GS	IP	H	HR	BB/9	K/9	K	GB%	BABIP
2017	SWB	AAA	26	2	1	0	5	5	26^{2}	32	1	3.7	11.1	33	53%	.397
2017	NYA	MLB	26	5	0	0	40	1	69	34	4	2.2	13.4	103	28%	.236
2018	NYA	MLB	27	8	3	0	63	0	75^{2}	64	9	1.8	11.2	94	33%	.307
2019	SWB	AAA	28	0	0	0	3	3	7^{1}	5	0	2.5	17.2	14	31%	.385
2019	NYA	MLB	28	4	4	2	54	15	69	66	10	2.5	12.8	98	36%	.346
2020	*NYA*	*MLB*	*29*	*3*	*3*	*0*	*61*	*0*	*65*	*53*	*9*	*2.8*	*12.1*	*87*	*35%*	*.301*

Comparables: Mike Clevinger, Gonzalez Germen, Mike Hauschild

Sometimes a trip down to Triple-A is crucial and beneficial for everyone involved. No one's a better example of that than Green. After allowing an eighth-inning grand slam to Justin Bour on April 23, his ERA was a whopping 16.43. Calling it a rough start would be offensive to rough starts. Outside of the big stage, he was able to zero in on his issues—a balance adjustment and relocating his fastball helped Green find his rhythm again, and expanded his role to the Yankees' go-to opener. Relying heavily on his four-seamer again, but mixing in his slider more frequently than last season turned out to be the key to his success. Whether he's used as an opener or a more traditional reliever in 2020, Green will once again be a key cog in the Yankee bullpen.

YEAR	TEAM	LVL	AGE	WHIP	ERA	DRA	WARP	MPH	FB%	WHF	CSP
2017	SWB	AAA	26	1.61	4.72	5.48	0.1				
2017	NYA	MLB	26	0.74	1.83	2.42	2.1	97.6	69.4	16.4	50.3
2018	NYA	MLB	27	1.04	2.50	3.38	1.3	97.8	86.6	14.9	52.6
2019	SWB	AAA	28	0.95	2.45	2.06	0.3				
2019	NYA	MLB	28	1.23	4.17	3.71	1.3	98.1	77.3	15	50.5
2020	*NYA*	*MLB*	*29*	*1.12*	*3.02*	*3.48*	*1.2*	*97.2*	*78.6*	*15.3*	*51.1*

Chad Green, continued

Pitch Shape vs LHH

Pitch Shape vs RHH

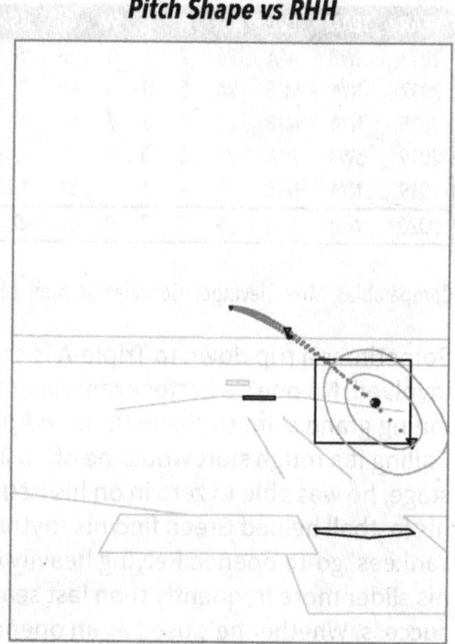

Type	Frequency	Velocity	H Movement	V Movement
● Fastball	77.3%	96.6 [112]	-6.1 [103]	-10.8 [113]
□ Sinker				
+ Cutter				
▲ Changeup				
✕ Splitter				
▽ Slider	21.3%	87.8 [114]	3 [92]	-29.6 [110]
◇ Curveball				
✥ Slow Curveball				
✱ Knuckleball				
▼ Screwball				

David Hale RHP

Born: 09/27/87 Age: 32 Bats: R Throws: R

Height: 6'2" Weight: 210 Origin: Round 3, 2009 Draft (#87 overall)

YEAR	TEAM	LVL	AGE	W	L	SV	G	GS	IP	H	HR	BB/9	K/9	K	GB%	BABIP
2017	TUL	AA	29	3	0	0	6	5	29	36	3	2.2	6.5	21	52%	.344
2017	OKL	AAA	29	2	4	0	9	9	52^2	64	4	1.2	6.7	39	45%	.347
2018	SWB	AAA	30	3	2	0	11	11	55^2	58	5	2.7	7.1	44	48%	.306
2018	MIN	MLB	30	0	0	0	1	0	3	4	1	12.0	6.0	2	40%	.333
2018	NYA	MLB	30	0	0	0	3	0	10^2	12	2	0.8	5.1	6	42%	.278
2019	SWB	AAA	31	3	2	0	7	7	32^2	36	3	2.8	8.3	30	54%	.330
2019	NYA	MLB	31	3	0	2	20	0	37^2	39	2	1.7	5.5	23	51%	.298
2020	*NYA*	*MLB*	*32*	*2*	*2*	*0*	*33*	*0*	*35*	*36*	*5*	*2.9*	*6.5*	*25*	*49%*	*.289*

Comparables: Chris Rusin, Stephen Fife, Jason Berken

The 32-year-old minor-league vet has been through a Hale of a ride. He's been DFA'd so many times the 'D' may as well stand for David, but his dream never faltered. That dedication led him to a resurgent season in the Bronx where he pitched surprisingly well in almost entirely low-leverage situations, but the second half of the year was less kind to the former Princeton Tiger. A combination of lumbar and knee injuries sidelined him for most of August and September, only to come back and be DFA'd in the middle of the playoffs to make room for Aaron Hicks on the ALCS roster. On top of all that, his Google search results tanked as David Hale, the diplomat and the U.S. Under Secretary of State for Political Affairs, testified in Donald Trump's impeachment inquiry in November.

YEAR	TEAM	LVL	AGE	WHIP	ERA	DRA	WARP	MPH	FB%	WHF	CSP
2017	TUL	AA	29	1.48	3.72	5.58	-0.2				
2017	OKL	AAA	29	1.35	4.27	4.34	0.8				
2018	SWB	AAA	30	1.35	4.20	4.57	0.6				
2018	MIN	MLB	30	2.67	12.00	5.89	0.0	93.7	49.1	10.5	38.3
2018	NYA	MLB	30	1.22	2.53	6.08	-0.1	94.0	49.1	12.4	48.6
2019	SWB	AAA	31	1.41	4.13	4.39	0.7				
2019	NYA	MLB	31	1.22	3.11	4.60	0.3	95.2	60.5	8.5	47.9
2020	*NYA*	*MLB*	*32*	*1.36*	*4.55*	*4.72*	*0.2*	*94.0*	*57.4*	*9.2*	*46.6*

David Hale, continued

Pitch Shape vs LHH | **Pitch Shape vs RHH**

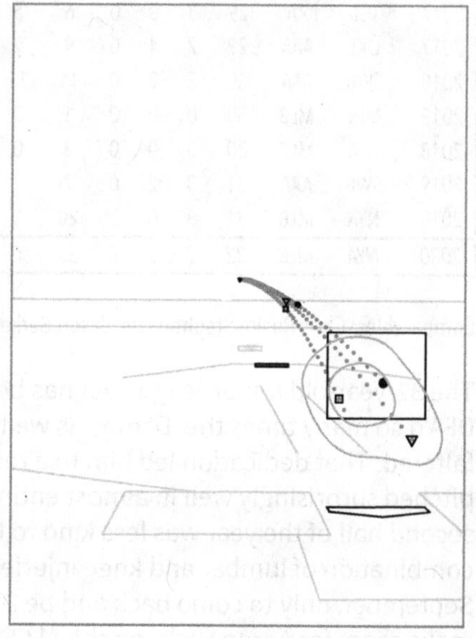

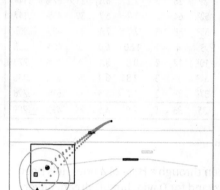

Type	Frequency	Velocity	H Movement	V Movement
● Fastball	33.4%	93.8 [104]	-7.6 [97]	-17 [97]
□ Sinker	27.1%	93.2 [103]	-13.3 [96]	-20.2 [101]
+ Cutter				
▲ Changeup	21.1%	82.3 [89]	-11.9 [97]	-28.1 [98]
✕ Splitter				
▽ Slider	18.4%	82.2 [91]	5.7 [103]	-35.4 [93]
◇ Curveball				
⊕ Slow Curveball				
✱ Knuckleball				
▼ Screwball				

J.A. Happ LHP

Born: 10/19/82 Age: 37 Bats: L Throws: L
Height: 6'5" Weight: 205 Origin: Round 3, 2004 Draft (#92 overall)

YEAR	TEAM	LVL	AGE	W	L	SV	G	GS	IP	H	HR	BB/9	K/9	K	GB%	BABIP
2017	TOR	MLB	34	10	11	0	25	25	145^1	145	18	2.8	8.8	142	48%	.302
2018	TOR	MLB	35	10	6	0	20	20	114	99	17	2.8	10.3	130	45%	.285
2018	NYA	MLB	35	7	0	0	11	11	63^2	51	10	2.3	8.9	63	33%	.250
2019	NYA	MLB	36	12	8	0	31	30	161^1	160	34	2.7	7.8	140	41%	.281
2020	*NYA*	*MLB*	*37*	*9*	*6*	*0*	*23*	*23*	*113*	*110*	*20*	*2.9*	*8.0*	*101*	*41%*	*.280*

Comparables: Jorge De La Rosa, Chuck Finley, Ted Lilly

Happ is a Dodge Neon. Not the car you want, but one that will get you from Point A to Point B. Just when the tank seems empty, he keeps chugging along, somehow, someway. He's dependable, good never great, and can take a beating. Nearly 200,000 miles on him, and Happ's still going. The squad's biggest victim of the juiced ball, he's a fifth starter these days, and he's okay with that. Neons are underrated.

YEAR	TEAM	LVL	AGE	WHIP	ERA	DRA	WARP	MPH	FB%	WHF	CSP
2017	TOR	MLB	34	1.31	3.53	4.07	2.4	94.4	71.3	10.5	43.8
2018	TOR	MLB	35	1.18	4.18	3.89	1.9	94.7	74.2	11.7	48
2018	NYA	MLB	35	1.05	2.69	4.00	1.0	94.0	72.3	11.1	48.3
2019	NYA	MLB	36	1.30	4.91	6.00	-0.4	93.6	68.3	11.3	47.3
2020	*NYA*	*MLB*	*37*	*1.29*	*4.24*	*4.61*	*1.2*	*92.7*	*69.2*	*10.9*	*45.6*

J.A. Happ, continued

Pitch Shape vs LHH

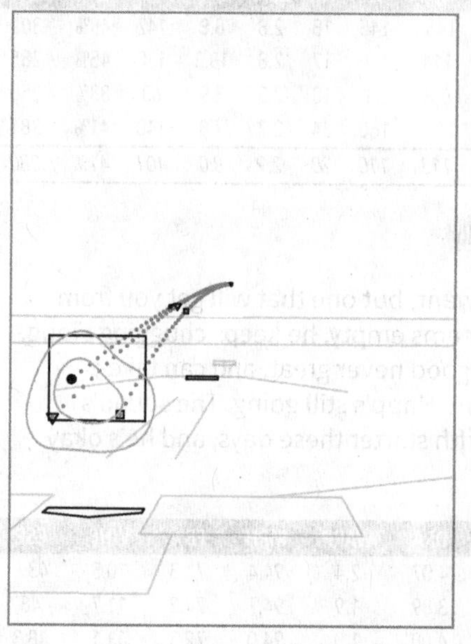

Pitch Shape vs RHH

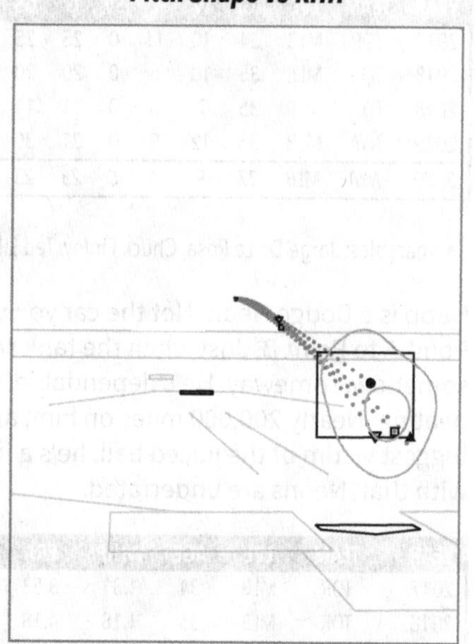

Type	Frequency	Velocity	H Movement	V Movement
● Fastball	48.6%	92.2 [99]	7.3 [98]	-13.7 [106]
□ Sinker	19.7%	89.6 [84]	12.4 [101]	-22.9 [91]
+ Cutter				
▲ Changeup	13.5%	86 [103]	13.1 [91]	-26.2 [104]
✕ Splitter				
▽ Slider	17.4%	84.9 [102]	-2.1 [88]	-28.4 [114]
◇ Curveball				
◈ Slow Curveball				
✱ Knuckleball				
▼ Screwball				

Jonathan Holder RHP

Born: 06/09/93 Age: 27 Bats: R Throws: R

Height: 6'2" Weight: 235 Origin: Round 6, 2014 Draft (#182 overall)

YEAR	TEAM	LVL	AGE	W	L	SV	G	GS	IP	H	HR	BB/9	K/9	K	GB%	BABIP
2017	SWB	AAA	24	0	0	1	12	0	16	15	1	4.5	11.8	21	40%	.359
2017	NYA	MLB	24	1	1	0	37	0	39^1	45	5	1.8	9.2	40	42%	.348
2018	SWB	AAA	25	1	0	0	4	1	6	5	1	1.5	12.0	8	53%	.286
2018	NYA	MLB	25	1	3	0	60	1	66	53	4	2.6	8.2	60	31%	.261
2019	SWB	AAA	26	1	1	2	9	0	12^1	13	1	1.5	10.9	15	49%	.353
2019	NYA	MLB	26	5	2	0	34	1	41^1	43	8	2.4	10.0	46	38%	.307
2020	*NYA*	*MLB*	*27*	*1*	*1*	*0*	*20*	*0*	*22*	*19*	*3*	*2.4*	*8.7*	*21*	*37%*	*.278*

Comparables: Sam Tuivailala, Jensen Lewis, Michael Tonkin

In the world of situational comedies, sometimes actors get replaced and the show in question doesn't comment on it. At all. They rarely look anything like the previous portrayer of the character, and viewers are simply forced to accept it. Every time Aaron Boone made a call to the bullpen for Holder in a high-leverage situation, the replacement came out. The Holder of the last two seasons was no more, instead an inferior one whose timing never quite clicked. A slight downtick in velocity from both his fastball and slider, the pitches he throws most often, paired with more pitches in the zone made for a dangerous combination—especially with such a homer-prone ball. Holder spent some time in Triple-A attempting to fix his issues, before an injury ended his season. Recasts never work out.

YEAR	TEAM	LVL	AGE	WHIP	ERA	DRA	WARP	MPH	FB%	WHF	CSP
2017	SWB	AAA	24	1.44	1.69	3.91	0.2				
2017	NYA	MLB	24	1.35	3.89	3.11	0.9	93.7	37.2	13.2	47.9
2018	SWB	AAA	25	1.00	3.00	2.94	0.2				
2018	NYA	MLB	25	1.09	3.14	4.33	0.5	94.4	55.4	11.5	47.5
2019	SWB	AAA	26	1.22	2.92	3.21	0.4				
2019	NYA	MLB	26	1.31	6.31	4.72	0.3	93.9	54.5	12.7	49.6
2020	*NYA*	*MLB*	*27*	*1.17*	*3.47*	*3.95*	*0.3*	*93.6*	*51.9*	*12.4*	*49*

Jonathan Holder, continued

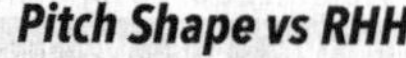

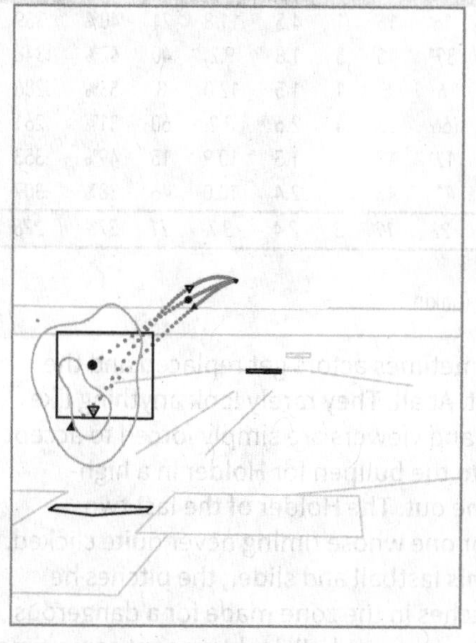

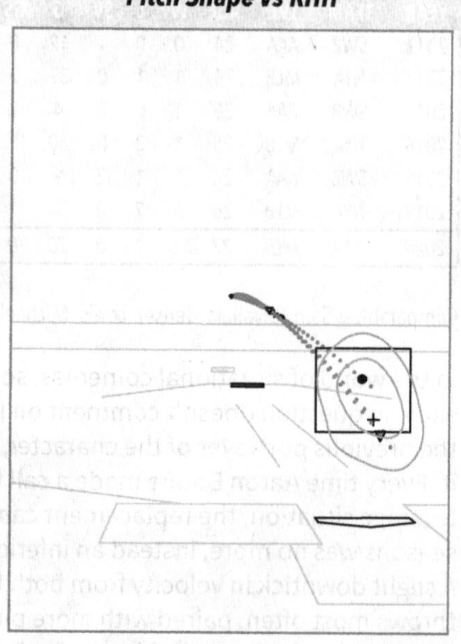

Type	Frequency	Velocity	H Movement	V Movement
● Fastball	54.5%	92.6 [100]	-2.4 [120]	-13.9 [105]
□ Sinker				
+ Cutter	5.1%	85 [77]	3.4 [109]	-31.2 [74]
▲ Changeup	16.5%	86.5 [104]	-12.7 [93]	-26.3 [103]
✕ Splitter				
▽ Slider	23.8%	81.1 [86]	10.3 [122]	-41.4 [76]
◇ Curveball				
⊕ Slow Curveball				
✱ Knuckleball				
▼ Screwball				

Tommy Kahnle RHP

Born: 08/07/89 Age: 30 Bats: R Throws: R

Height: 6'1" Weight: 235 Origin: Round 5, 2010 Draft (#175 overall)

YEAR	TEAM	LVL	AGE	W	L	SV	G	GS	IP	H	HR	BB/9	K/9	K	GB%	BABIP
2017	CHA	MLB	27	1	3	0	37	0	36	28	3	1.8	15.0	60	43%	.352
2017	NYA	MLB	27	1	1	0	32	0	26^2	25	1	3.4	12.1	36	40%	.364
2018	SWB	AAA	28	2	2	1	25	0	24^2	23	2	4.0	13.5	37	40%	.375
2018	NYA	MLB	28	2	0	1	24	0	23^1	23	3	5.8	11.6	30	39%	.339
2019	NYA	MLB	29	3	2	0	72	0	61^1	45	9	2.9	12.9	88	51%	.279
2020	*NYA*	*MLB*	*30*	*3*	*3*	*0*	*56*	*0*	*60*	*46*	*6*	*4.0*	*12.5*	*83*	*47%*	*.299*

Comparables: Jordan Jankowski, Chasen Shreve, J.J. Hoover

Tommy thunder thighs. Tommy tight pants. Tommy two times. Tommy throwing straight fire. Kahnle's a lunatic, in a great way. A former Red-Bull-chugging, would-tackle-a-bear-for-an-out, crazy man who turned things around after a mess of a previous season. The righty reliever quickly returned to his 2017 form, becoming a vital piece in the bullpen when injuries and ineffectiveness plagued his teammates. The secret to Kahnle's success was relying heavily on his changeup, which he threw 52 percent of the time, allowing him to almost eliminate his slider completely. Regaining a tick on his fastball after watching the pitch fall flat in 2018 didn't hurt either. He was at home in the late innings, his aggressive sprints from the bullpen and dousing of himself in bottled water added much needed dramatic effect to his game. Kahnle's going to stay in the exact same late-inning role for at least another two years.

YEAR	TEAM	LVL	AGE	WHIP	ERA	DRA	WARP	MPH	FB%	WHF	CSP
2017	CHA	MLB	27	0.97	2.50	2.10	1.2	100.2	72.6	18.2	51.3
2017	NYA	MLB	27	1.31	2.70	2.05	0.9	99.4	58.9	17.2	46.6
2018	SWB	AAA	28	1.38	4.01	4.05	0.3				
2018	NYA	MLB	28	1.63	6.56	4.03	0.2	97.2	54.3	15.2	46
2019	NYA	MLB	29	1.06	3.67	2.41	2.0	98.6	44.1	18.6	46.6
2020	*NYA*	*MLB*	*30*	*1.21*	*2.95*	*3.30*	*1.2*	*98.0*	*52.6*	*17.7*	*46.9*

Tommy Kahnle, continued

Pitch Shape vs LHH

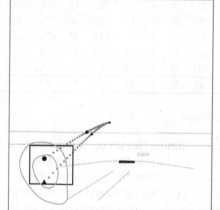

Pitch Shape vs RHH

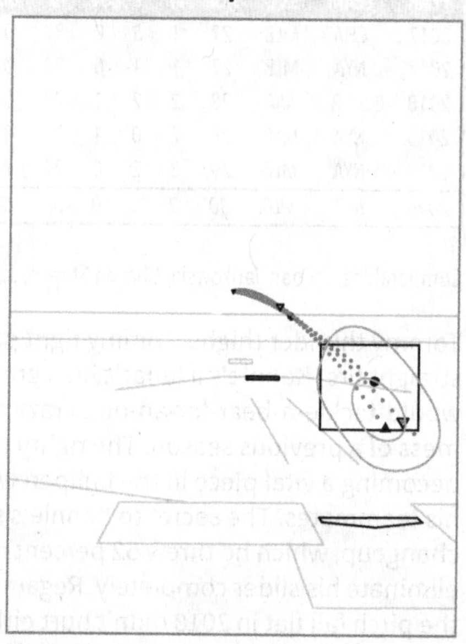

Type	Frequency	Velocity	H Movement	V Movement
● Fastball	44.1%	96.8 [113]	-5.8 [105]	-12.4 [109]
□ Sinker				
+ Cutter				
▲ Changeup	52.0%	90.2 [118]	-12.4 [94]	-26.2 [103]
✕ Splitter				
▽ Slider	3.9%	83.6 [97]	7.6 [111]	-34.9 [95]
◇ Curveball				
⊕ Slow Curveball				
✱ Knuckleball				
▼ Screwball				

Adam Ottavino RHP

Born: 11/22/85 Age: 34 Bats: B Throws: R
Height: 6'5" Weight: 220 Origin: Round 1, 2006 Draft (#30 overall)

YEAR	TEAM	LVL	AGE	W	L	SV	G	GS	IP	H	HR	BB/9	K/9	K	GB%	BABIP
2017	COL	MLB	31	2	3	0	63	0	53^1	48	8	6.6	10.6	63	40%	.310
2018	COL	MLB	32	6	4	6	75	0	77^2	41	5	4.2	13.0	112	44%	.242
2019	NYA	MLB	33	6	5	2	73	0	66^1	47	5	5.4	11.9	88	41%	.286
2020	*NYA*	*MLB*	*34*	*3*	*3*	*3*	*61*	*0*	*65*	*51*	*9*	*4.2*	*11.4*	*82*	*43%*	*.281*

Comparables: David Hernandez, Kyle Farnsworth, Al Reyes

Superstitions are a major part of baseball, like hot dogs and the seventh inning stretch; the game is equally linked to the occasionally insane superstitious actions of its players. Avoiding the chalk lines, refusing to change articles of clothing after a win, slump-busting facial hair. Ottavino's personal superstition involves switching Gatorade colors if he's having trouble. It's time to add "don't insult baseball legends" to his list. When Ottavino shared a story in which he claimed he'd strike out Babe Ruth every time, he got himself in hot water and picked up some serious bad juju. Sure, it was taken out of context. And yes, it makes sense with the way the game has evolved that someone who played in the olden times wouldn't be able to handle the harsh movement of Ottavino's sweeping slider. But it's Babe Ruth. Ottavino was a dominant bullpen arm throughout the regular season because the Great Bambino let him be. But once October hit, he lost all effectiveness and Yankees fans went from cheering in support to screaming Ottavino get off the mound-o. During four of his postseason appearances, he failed to record a single out. You don't mess with the Colossus of Clout, and the hard throwing righty paid the price when it hurt the most.

YEAR	TEAM	LVL	AGE	WHIP	ERA	DRA	WARP	MPH	FB%	WHF	CSP
2017	COL	MLB	31	1.63	5.06	6.10	-0.6	96.6	50.2	9.9	46.3
2018	COL	MLB	32	0.99	2.43	3.02	1.7	96.3	43.1	13	47.9
2019	NYA	MLB	33	1.31	1.90	3.63	1.2	95.7	41.6	11.8	48.5
2020	*NYA*	*MLB*	*34*	*1.25*	*3.45*	*3.71*	*1.0*	*95.0*	*43.4*	*11.6*	*47*

Adam Ottavino, continued

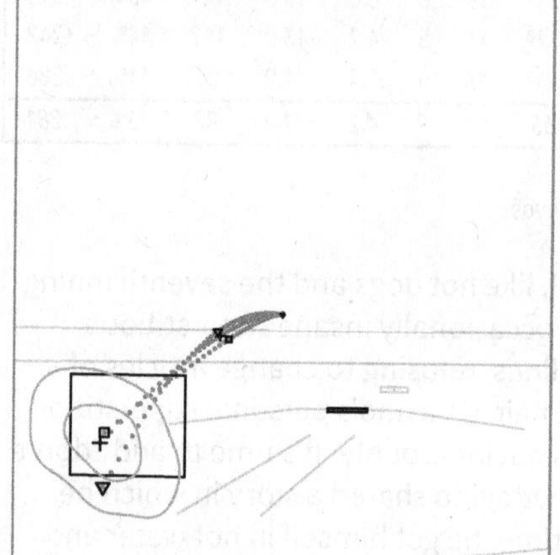

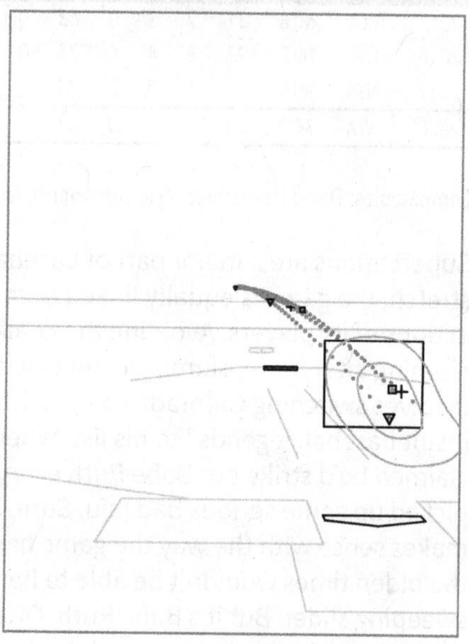

Type	Frequency	Velocity	H Movement	V Movement
● Fastball				
□ Sinker	39.9%	94.2 [108]	-13.1 [97]	-21.2 [97]
+ Cutter	13.4%	88.6 [100]	2.8 [106]	-23 [104]
▲ Changeup				
✕ Splitter				
▽ Slider	45.0%	82.1 [90]	16.6 [149]	-35.9 [92]
◇ Curveball				
⊕ Slow Curveball				
✱ Knuckleball				
▼ Screwball				

James Paxton LHP

Born: 11/06/88 Age: 31 Bats: L Throws: L
Height: 6'4" Weight: 235 Origin: Round 4, 2010 Draft (#132 overall)

YEAR	TEAM	LVL	AGE	W	L	SV	G	GS	IP	H	HR	BB/9	K/9	K	GB%	BABIP
2017	SEA	MLB	28	12	5	0	24	24	136	113	9	2.4	10.3	156	46%	.300
2018	SEA	MLB	29	11	6	0	28	28	160[1]	134	23	2.4	11.7	208	41%	.299
2019	NYA	MLB	30	15	6	0	29	29	150[2]	138	23	3.3	11.1	186	40%	.313
2020	*NYA*	*MLB*	*31*	*11*	*6*	*0*	*26*	*26*	*143*	*123*	*19*	*3.3*	*11.0*	*174*	*41%*	*.301*

Comparables: David Price, Kyle Lobstein, Jaime García

The Big Maple takes the Big Apple. It sounds like a Mary-Kate and Ashley movie, which is fitting for Paxton's first season in the Bronx because the majority of his starts included what must have been a zany twin switch between the first and second innings. Mary-Kate was running late, so Ashley threw on the uniform to stall. Paxton's first-inning ERA was a whopping 9.00, giving up 12 of his 23 homers on the entire season during that frame. Thankfully, Mary-Kate always made it there in time for the second and dominated the way that was expected throughout the rest of the start. With one year left until the 31-year-old hits free agency, he'll look to build on his strong close to the season—opposing hitters scratched out a .177/.248/.298 line against the left-hander during August and September—in 2020 to try to bring in that Olsen-level cash.

YEAR	TEAM	LVL	AGE	WHIP	ERA	DRA	WARP	MPH	FB%	WHF	CSP
2017	SEA	MLB	28	1.10	2.98	2.63	4.5	98.1	65.6	13.5	49.5
2018	SEA	MLB	29	1.10	3.76	2.67	4.9	98.0	63.7	15.8	53
2019	NYA	MLB	30	1.28	3.82	4.18	2.6	97.6	60	15.3	47
2020	*NYA*	*MLB*	*31*	*1.23*	*3.38*	*3.73*	*2.9*	*97.0*	*62.1*	*15*	*49.3*

James Paxton, continued

Pitch Shape vs LHH

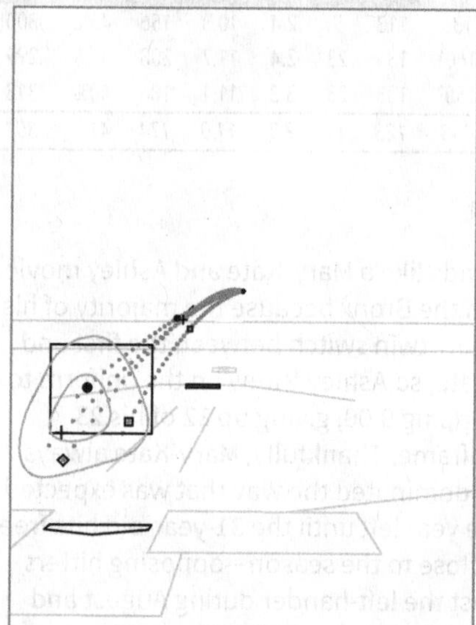

Pitch Shape vs RHH

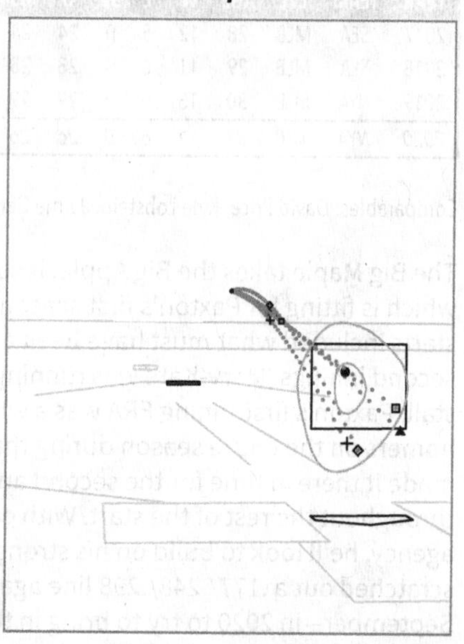

Type	Frequency	Velocity	H Movement	V Movement
● Fastball	53.7%	95.7 [109]	9.7 [87]	-12.8 [108]
□ Sinker	6.2%	95.1 [113]	14.3 [89]	-16.7 [113]
+ Cutter	20.2%	88.3 [97]	-1.4 [97]	-27.2 [88]
▲ Changeup				
✕ Splitter				
▽ Slider				
◇ Curveball	18.6%	81.2 [109]	-2.8 [81]	-43.5 [109]
⊕ Slow Curveball				
✱ Knuckleball				
▼ Screwball				

CC Sabathia LHP

Born: 07/21/80 Age: 39 Bats: L Throws: L
Height: 6'6" Weight: 300 Origin: Round 1, 1998 Draft (#20 overall)

YEAR	TEAM	LVL	AGE	W	L	SV	G	GS	IP	H	HR	BB/9	K/9	K	GB%	BABIP
2017	NYA	MLB	36	14	5	0	27	27	148^{2}	139	21	3.0	7.3	120	51%	.276
2018	NYA	MLB	37	9	7	0	29	29	153	150	19	3.0	8.2	140	45%	.295
2019	NYA	MLB	38	5	8	0	23	22	107^{1}	112	27	3.3	9.0	107	41%	.292
2020	*NYA*	*MLB*	*39*	*2*	*2*	*0*	*33*	*0*	*35*	*35*	*7*	*3.2*	*8.7*	*34*	*42%*	*.294*

Comparables: Steve Carlton, Frank Tanana, Kevin Millwood

A future first-ballot Hall of Famer, Sabathia's final season was somewhat of a victory lap. If there was ever any doubt about whether deserves the highest honor in the game, reaching 3,000 strikeouts, getting 250 wins and literally pitching until his arm gave out put them to rest. Sabathia's the last of his kind, a dying breed of pitchers who'd put their neck on the line for their team, who used his voice for those who couldn't use theirs. The player he was on the mound—a leader, a fighter—was the same man he was off the field. Sabathia's season wasn't perfect by any statistical standard. He gave up too many home runs and he didn't pitch deep enough in games. For Sabathia, what he meant to his communities, to the game and to the Bronx was bigger than baseball too.

YEAR	TEAM	LVL	AGE	WHIP	ERA	DRA	WARP	MPH	FB%	WHF	CSP
2017	NYA	MLB	36	1.27	3.69	3.92	2.7	93.0	53.2	9.6	45.3
2018	NYA	MLB	37	1.31	3.65	4.40	1.6	92.0	59.1	11.8	45.7
2019	NYA	MLB	38	1.41	4.95	6.41	-0.7	90.9	57.6	11.9	45.3
2020	*NYA*	*MLB*	*39*	*1.36*	*4.77*	*4.87*	*0.1*	*90.3*	*55.3*	*10.9*	*44*

CC Sabathia, continued

Pitch Shape vs LHH

Pitch Shape vs RHH

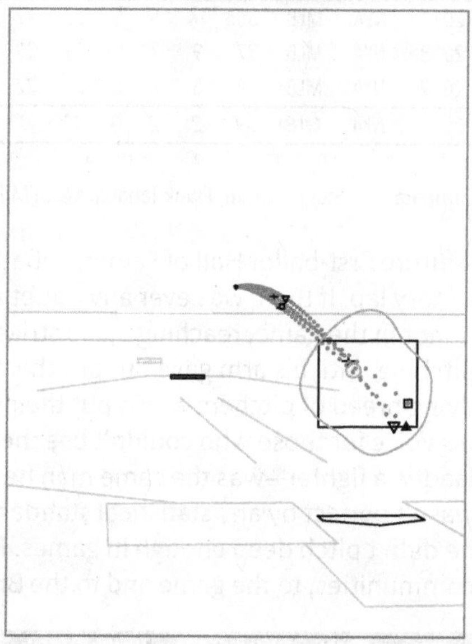

Type	Frequency	Velocity	H Movement	V Movement
● Fastball				
□ Sinker	14.5%	89.5 [84]	12.1 [104]	-22.9 [91]
+ Cutter	42.6%	88.7 [100]	0.2 [88]	-21.5 [109]
▲ Changeup	12.3%	83 [92]	8.1 [114]	-28.3 [98]
✕ Splitter				
▽ Slider	30.2%	79.5 [79]	-9.5 [119]	-37.6 [87]
◇ Curveball				
⊕ Slow Curveball				
✱ Knuckleball				
▼ Screwball				

Luis Severino RHP

Born: 02/20/94 Age: 26 Bats: R Throws: R
Height: 6'2" Weight: 215 Origin: International Free Agent, 2011

YEAR	TEAM	LVL	AGE	W	L	SV	G	GS	IP	H	HR	BB/9	K/9	K	GB%	BABIP
2017	NYA	MLB	23	14	6	0	31	31	193^{1}	150	21	2.4	10.7	230	50%	.272
2018	NYA	MLB	24	19	8	0	32	32	191^{1}	173	19	2.2	10.3	220	42%	.314
2019	NYA	MLB	25	1	1	0	3	3	12	6	0	4.5	12.8	17	38%	.250
2020	*NYA*	*MLB*	*26*	*12*	*6*	*0*	*26*	*26*	*156*	*130*	*20*	*3.0*	*10.6*	*184*	*43%*	*.288*

Comparables: Yovani Gallardo, Tommy Hanson, Carlos Martínez

First, the bad news. The young ace didn't make his first start of the season until September 17th, after being sidelined first with shoulder inflammation, and then a grade-two lat strain. The good news? The version of Severino who made his triumphant return looked a lot like the elite starter they severely missed during the majority of the regular season. The Yankees kept him on a strict pitch count, never letting him go more than five innings. His high-90s velocity was there from the jump, topping out at 98 in his first start back. The lone laggard was the command of his secondary pitches, which was the driver of his elevated walk rate over the small sample, but you can excuse a pitcher for being a touch rusty after missing over six months of action. Expect a repeat of the All-Star-caliber Severino come 2020.

YEAR	TEAM	LVL	AGE	WHIP	ERA	DRA	WARP	MPH	FB%	WHF	CSP
2017	NYA	MLB	23	1.04	2.98	2.68	6.2	99.6	51.4	13.7	49.4
2018	NYA	MLB	24	1.14	3.39	2.79	5.6	99.7	50.5	13.3	51.2
2019	NYA	MLB	25	1.00	1.50	4.05	0.2	98.0	56.6	12.8	47.3
2020	*NYA*	*MLB*	*26*	*1.17*	*3.12*	*3.52*	*3.5*	*99.2*	*52*	*13.7*	*50*

Luis Severino, continued

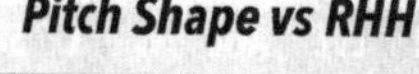

Pitch Shape vs LHH

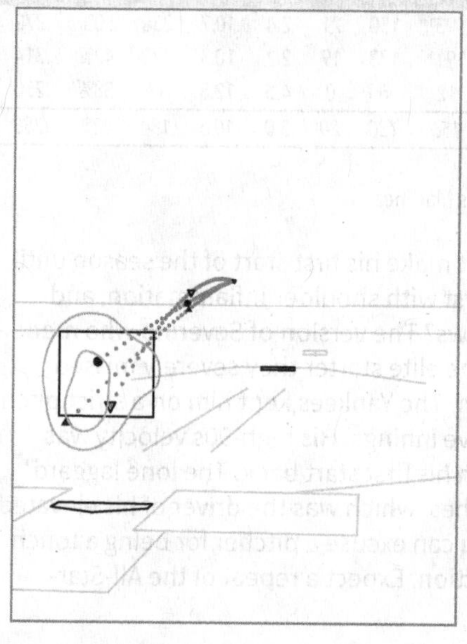

Pitch Shape vs RHH

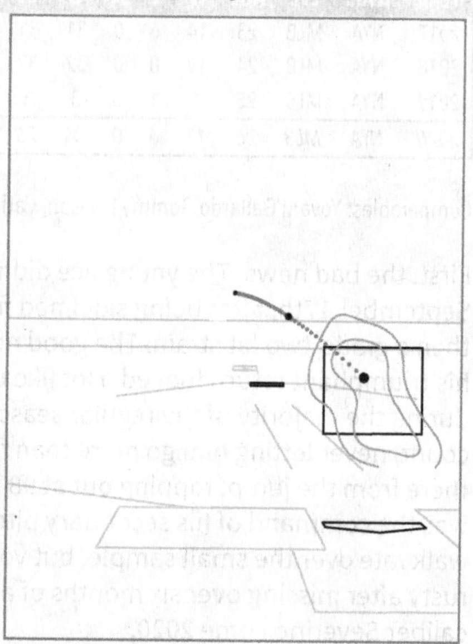

Type	Frequency	Velocity	H Movement	V Movement
● Fastball	56.6%	96 [110]	-6.6 [101]	-12.2 [110]
□ Sinker				
+ Cutter				
▲ Changeup	16.4%	88.1 [110]	-11.8 [97]	-24.1 [110]
× Splitter				
▽ Slider	26.9%	83.9 [98]	9.5 [119]	-37.8 [87]
◇ Curveball				
⊕ Slow Curveball				
✱ Knuckleball				
▼ Screwball				

Masahiro Tanaka RHP

Born: 11/01/88 Age: 31 Bats: R Throws: R
Height: 6'3" Weight: 215 Origin: International Free Agent, 2014

YEAR	TEAM	LVL	AGE	W	L	SV	G	GS	IP	H	HR	BB/9	K/9	K	GB%	BABIP
2017	NYA	MLB	28	13	12	0	30	30	178^{1}	180	35	2.1	9.8	194	50%	.306
2018	NYA	MLB	29	12	6	0	27	27	156	141	25	2.0	9.2	159	49%	.284
2019	NYA	MLB	30	11	9	0	32	31	182	186	28	2.0	7.4	149	48%	.293
2020	*NYA*	*MLB*	*31*	*11*	*7*	*0*	*28*	*28*	*151*	*149*	*28*	*2.3*	*8.0*	*135*	*48%*	*.282*

Comparables: Michael Pineda, Matt Harvey, Ricky Nolasco

Tanaka is a big-game pitcher, and when the Yankees need him to show up, he goes to heroic lengths to do so. His postseason numbers are ridiculous, with an ERA of 1.76 across eight starts, and he had never given up more than two runs in a single one of them until Game 4 of last year's ALCS against the Astros. However, his domination of the division-rival Rays also helped the Yankees wrap up their first AL East title since 2012. In his four starts against them, Tanaka had a 1.59 ERA and 28 strikeouts against just three walks, including a June complete-game shutout. Going into his age-31 season and the final year of his $155-million contract, Tanaka may be overshadowed by the Gerrit Cole signing but is a strong leader in his own right and poised to take that mantle after CC Sabathia's retirement.

YEAR	TEAM	LVL	AGE	WHIP	ERA	DRA	WARP	MPH	FB%	WHF	CSP
2017	NYA	MLB	28	1.24	4.74	3.91	3.3	94.3	37.6	15.8	41.7
2018	NYA	MLB	29	1.13	3.75	3.95	2.5	93.9	31.5	14.8	44
2019	NYA	MLB	30	1.24	4.45	4.94	1.6	93.6	32.5	11.7	46.8
2020	*NYA*	*MLB*	*31*	*1.24*	*4.13*	*4.55*	*1.7*	*93.0*	*33.3*	*13.6*	*44.3*

Masahiro Tanaka, continued

Pitch Shape vs LHH

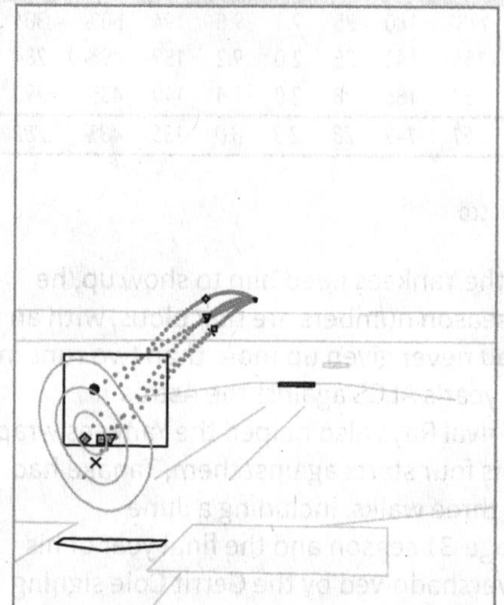

Pitch Shape vs RHH

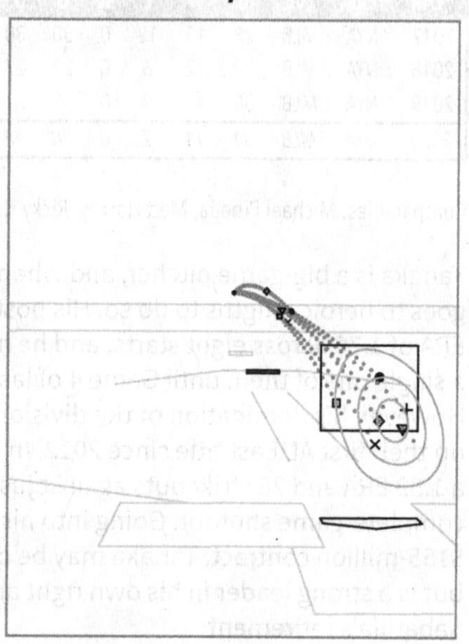

Type	Frequency	Velocity	H Movement	V Movement
● Fastball	27.0%	91.7 [98]	-8.7 [92]	-15.2 [102]
□ Sinker	3.9%	90.6 [90]	-13.1 [97]	-22.1 [94]
+ Cutter				
▲ Changeup				
× Splitter	28.0%	87 [108]	-10.9 [89]	-27.6 [105]
▽ Slider	36.2%	83.4 [96]	5.9 [104]	-34.6 [96]
◇ Curveball	3.2%	76.2 [92]	8 [102]	-50.2 [95]
⊕ Slow Curveball				
✱ Knuckleball				
▼ Screwball				

PLAYER COMMENTS WITHOUT GRAPHS

Miguel Andújar 3B

Born: 03/02/95 Age: 25 Bats: R Throws: R
Height: 6'0" Weight: 215 Origin: International Free Agent, 2011

YEAR	TEAM	LVL	AGE	PA	R	2B	3B	HR	RBI	BB	K	SB	CS	AVG/OBP/SLG
2017	TRN	AA	22	272	30	23	1	7	52	12	38	2	3	.312/.342/.494
2017	SWB	AAA	22	250	36	13	1	9	30	17	33	3	0	.317/.364/.502
2017	NYA	MLB	22	8	0	2	0	0	4	1	0	1	0	.571/.625/.857
2018	NYA	MLB	23	606	83	47	2	27	92	25	97	2	1	.297/.328/.527
2019	NYA	MLB	24	49	1	0	0	0	1	1	11	0	0	.128/.143/.128
2020	*NYA*	*MLB*	*25*	*455*	*51*	*25*	*2*	*20*	*62*	*22*	*87*	*2*	*1*	*.257/.299/.459*

Comparables: Brandon Drury, Jeimer Candelario, Cheslor Cuthbert

As the Rookie of the Year runner-up in 2018, there was more pressure on Andújar than anyone to carry that success across calendar years. Yet a season almost entirely lost to injury did little to answer the long-term questions that surround the 25-year-old. In the shadow of a presumed move to another corner (or designated hitter) coming, and a new breakout third baseman playing Ringo Starr to his Pete Best, Andújar enters 2020 with less pressure but a lot more uncertainty—starting with whether he'll even be ready to head north with the team on Opening Day after undergoing surgery to repair a torn labrum in his right shoulder last May.

YEAR	TEAM	LVL	AGE	PA	DRC+	VORP	BABIP	BRR	FRAA	WARP
2017	TRN	AA	22	272	126	18.8	.338	-1.6	3B(58): -4.5	1.0
2017	SWB	AAA	22	250	142	20.3	.333	0.3	3B(57): -1.4	1.7
2017	NYA	MLB	22	8	96	2.0	.571	0.0	3B(3): 0.0	0.0
2018	NYA	MLB	23	606	120	37.5	.316	-0.1	3B(136): -15.2	2.0
2019	NYA	MLB	24	49	63	-1.3	.162	0.2	3B(4): -0.8	-0.2
2020	*NYA*	*MLB*	*25*	*455*	*101*	*8.4*	*.281*	*0.0*	*3B -4*	*0.4*

Jasson Dominguez CF

Born: 02/07/03 Age: 17 Bats: B Throws: R
Height: 5'10" Weight: 190 Origin: International Free Agent, 2019

Talent takes human form in Dominguez. He's the Regina George of international signings; everyone wants him and those that don't, want to be him. The Yankees love dipping their toes in the international market, spending over $5 million on the switch-hitting outfielder from the Dominican Republic. He may be shorter than 6-foot but his tools have caused scouts to call him The Martian, as his skill set is not from this planet. Dominguez was named after former MVP and Yankee slugger Jason Giambi (seriously), but the comps so far have touched on such untouchable names as Mike Trout, Mickey Mantle and Bo Jackson. That gives you a pretty good sense of his power, speed and defensive upside. Dominguez is as far away as can be from the majors—he was born in 2003 for god's sake—but he's nearly a lock to make his stateside debut this summer, which will be must-watch viewing for the entire baseball world.

Estevan Florial CF

Born: 11/25/97 Age: 22 Bats: L Throws: R
Height: 6'1" Weight: 185 Origin: International Free Agent, 2015

YEAR	TEAM	LVL	AGE	PA	R	2B	3B	HR	RBI	BB	K	SB	CS	AVG/OBP/SLG
2017	CSC	A	19	389	64	21	5	11	43	41	124	17	7	.297/.373/.483
2017	TAM	A+	19	87	13	2	2	2	14	9	24	6	1	.303/.368/.461
2018	TAM	A+	20	339	45	16	3	3	27	44	87	11	10	.255/.354/.361
2019	TAM	A+	21	301	38	10	3	8	38	24	98	9	5	.237/.297/.383
2020	*NYA*	*MLB*	*22*	*35*	*3*	*2*	*0*	*1*	*4*	*3*	*13*	*1*	*0*	*.222/.280/.370*

Comparables: Lewis Brinson, Byron Buxton, Daniel Fields

Florial's injuries continue to disrupt crucial development time, as he's yet to get a full, healthy season in High-A under his belt. He still has the same four standout tools he showed up stateside with a few years ago—plus speed, plus power, a strong arm and reliable centerfield glove—but still hasn't racked up enough at-bats to correct his pitch recognition and general plate discipline issues. His ceiling remains high, though so do those strikeout rates.

YEAR	TEAM	LVL	AGE	PA	DRC+	VORP	BABIP	BRR	FRAA	WARP
2017	CSC	A	19	389	134	31.8	.431	-0.7	CF(62): -2.1, LF(13): 2.9	2.4
2017	TAM	A+	19	87	125	7.4	.404	0.7	CF(18): 0.4	0.6
2018	TAM	A+	20	339	103	10.5	.353	-0.9	CF(59): 1.8, RF(6): -0.2	1.1
2019	TAM	A+	21	301	92	4.2	.335	1.0	CF(62): 2.9	1.1
2020	*NYA*	*MLB*	*22*	*35*	*74*	*0.1*	*.344*	*0.0*	*CF 0*	*0.0*

Troy Tulowitzki SS

Born: 10/10/84 Age: 35 Bats: R Throws: R
Height: 6'3" Weight: 205 Origin: Round 1, 2005 Draft (#7 overall)

YEAR	TEAM	LVL	AGE	PA	R	2B	3B	HR	RBI	BB	K	SB	CS	AVG/OBP/SLG
2017	TOR	MLB	32	260	16	10	0	7	26	17	40	0	1	.249/.300/.378
2019	NYA	MLB	34	13	1	1	0	1	1	2	4	0	0	.182/.308/.545
2020	*NYA*	*MLB*	*35*	*251*	*31*	*10*	*0*	*11*	*34*	*22*	*57*	*1*	*0*	*.252/.326/.448*

Comparables: Jhonny Peralta, J.J. Hardy, Jay Bell

Seemingly on track for a Hall-of-Fame induction during his prime, the last few seasons of Tulowitzki's playing career were bizarre and fairly heartbreaking. The All-Star caliber player he was during his time in Colorado could never fight his way back from the injuries to reemerge again, despite how badly he wanted to stick it to the doubters. Luckily, he defied the odds long enough to sneak in a swan song before retiring for good. Tulo's first and only home run as a Yankee was an emotional one, as he rounded the bases with an expression on his face that looks to say "I'm finally back", and he's a bit choked up about it. The injury bug bit him once again shortly thereafter, and after years of pushing himself, he just couldn't anymore. Tulo's presence will be missed, but it's a fitting end to his story. He grew up idolizing Derek Jeter and he got to spend his last games on the field playing shortstop in pinstripes. How can you not be romantic about baseball?

YEAR	TEAM	LVL	AGE	PA	DRC+	VORP	BABIP	BRR	FRAA	WARP
2017	TOR	MLB	32	260	85	0.7	.272	-3.0	SS(64): 2.4	0.7
2019	NYA	MLB	34	13	74	0.2	.167	0.0	SS(4): 0.7	0.1
2020	*NYA*	*MLB*	*35*	*251*	*104*	*8.3*	*.288*	*-1.1*	*SS 1*	*0.9*

Anthony Volpe SS

Born: 04/28/01 Age: 19 Bats: R Throws: R
Height: 5'11" Weight: 180 Origin: Round 1, 2019 Draft (#30 overall)

YEAR	TEAM	LVL	AGE	PA	R	2B	3B	HR	RBI	BB	K	SB	CS	AVG/OBP/SLG
2019	PUL	RK+	18	150	19	7	2	2	11	23	38	6	1	.215/.349/.355
2020	*NYA*	*MLB*	*19*	*251*	*24*	*11*	*1*	*5*	*24*	*28*	*87*	*3*	*1*	*.209/.306/.338*

Nothing captivates the attention of New York baseball fans like a local boy who grew up rooting for the team making good on the promise of his future. There are quite a number of years standing between the introduction and the outcome with Volpe, but the New Jersey native and Yankee fan was bought out of a strong commitment to Vanderbilt after being taken towards the end of the first round in the 2019 draft. It's not the flashiest of profiles, but Volpe substitutes a dreamy upside for a steady hand across the board. In other words, you won't find any tools on his scouting report that start with a three or four, but you won't find any that start with a six or seven either.

YEAR	TEAM	LVL	AGE	PA	DRC+	VORP	BABIP	BRR	FRAA	WARP
2019	PUL	RK+	18	150	100	8.5	.289	0.3		0.7
2020	*NYA*	*MLB*	*19*	*251*	*78*	*1.0*	*.321*	*0.0*		*0.1*

Deivi Garcia RHP

Born: 05/19/99 Age: 21 Bats: R Throws: R
Height: 5'9" Weight: 163 Origin: International Free Agent, 2015

YEAR	TEAM	LVL	AGE	W	L	SV	G	GS	IP	H	HR	BB/9	K/9	K	GB%	BABIP
2017	DYA	RK	18	1	1	0	3	3	15^1	10	1	1.2	10.6	18	58%	.281
2017	YAT	RK	18	3	0	0	4	2	16^2	9	3	2.2	13.0	24	32%	.194
2017	PUL	RK	18	2	1	0	6	5	28	23	3	4.2	13.8	43	32%	.370
2018	CSC	A	19	2	4	0	8	8	40^2	31	5	2.2	13.9	63	31%	.302
2018	TAM	A+	19	2	0	0	5	5	28^1	19	0	2.5	11.1	35	37%	.292
2019	TAM	A+	20	0	2	0	4	4	17^2	14	0	4.1	16.8	33	50%	.438
2019	TRN	AA	20	4	4	0	11	11	53^2	43	2	4.4	14.6	87	44%	.360
2019	SWB	AAA	20	1	3	0	11	6	40	39	8	4.5	10.1	45	38%	.307
2020	*NYA*	*MLB*	*21*	*2*	*2*	*0*	*15*	*5*	*30*	*30*	*5*	*3.5*	*11.6*	*39*	*40%*	*.339*

Comparables: Sean Reid-Foley, David Holmberg, Alex Reyes

New York's farm system revolved around the rise of Garcia, who shot up the ranks and became their top prospect without much debate. The diminutive righty was exciting enough when he simply featured a fastball and curve that could each draw plus-plus grades. However, the 2019 season saw the continued development of his change and the addition of a suddenly plus slider to boot. Garcia would have likely made a late-season appearance in the big leagues, but an innings limit held him back—after all, his 111 1/3 innings were by far a career high. A smaller frame gives the impression his body won't hold up to the grueling workload of a starter, and he's going to need to cut back on the walks in order to get deep enough into games, but it's hard to argue with dominance.

YEAR	TEAM	LVL	AGE	WHIP	ERA	DRA	WARP	MPH	FB%	WHF	CSP
2017	DYA	RK	18	0.78	1.17	1.77	0.7				
2017	YAT	RK	18	0.78	3.24	1.42	0.8				
2017	PUL	RK	18	1.29	4.50	3.01	0.9				
2018	CSC	A	19	1.01	3.76	3.14	1.0				
2018	TAM	A+	19	0.95	1.27	2.69	0.9				
2019	TAM	A+	20	1.25	3.06	3.55	0.3				
2019	TRN	AA	20	1.29	3.86	4.30	0.4				
2019	SWB	AAA	20	1.48	5.40	5.12	0.6				
2020	*NYA*	*MLB*	*21*	*1.39*	*4.71*	*4.96*	*0.2*				

Jordan Montgomery LHP

Born: 12/27/92 Age: 27 Bats: L Throws: L
Height: 6'6" Weight: 225 Origin: Round 4, 2014 Draft (#122 overall)

YEAR	TEAM	LVL	AGE	W	L	SV	G	GS	IP	H	HR	BB/9	K/9	K	GB%	BABIP
2017	NYA	MLB	24	9	7	0	29	29	155[1]	140	21	3.0	8.3	144	42%	.275
2018	NYA	MLB	25	2	0	0	6	6	27[1]	25	3	4.0	7.6	23	46%	.282
2019	NYA	MLB	26	0	0	0	2	1	4	7	1	0.0	11.2	5	21%	.462
2020	*NYA*	*MLB*	*27*	*5*	*3*	*0*	*13*	*13*	*65*	*59*	*9*	*3.1*	*7.4*	*53*	*41%*	*.268*

Comparables: Sean Manaea, Steven Matz, Dan Straily

Recovering from Tommy John surgery was Montgomery's one and only goal in 2019. He was never expected to contribute to the team, in the postseason or otherwise, and if he didn't make it back in time for September call-ups no one would have cared. He made a couple appearances, threw some good pitches, mostly bad ones, and no real weight should be placed on either aside from his velocity staying intact. Montgomery will be competing for a spot in the rotation this year, and how quickly his command comes back will determine how successful that campaign is.

YEAR	TEAM	LVL	AGE	WHIP	ERA	DRA	WARP	MPH	FB%	WHF	CSP
2017	NYA	MLB	24	1.23	3.88	4.51	1.8	93.6	41.8	12.7	43
2018	NYA	MLB	25	1.35	3.62	5.86	-0.2	92.3	41.1	11	45.3
2019	NYA	MLB	26	1.75	6.75	6.11	0.0	93.4	50	13.4	49
2020	*NYA*	*MLB*	*27*	*1.26*	*3.75*	*4.19*	*1.0*	*92.9*	*42.5*	*12.5*	*46.8*

T.J. Sikkema LHP

Born: 07/25/98 Age: 21 Bats: L Throws: L
Height: 6'0" Weight: 221 Origin: Round 1, 2019 Draft (#38 overall)

YEAR	TEAM	LVL	AGE	W	L	SV	G	GS	IP	H	HR	BB/9	K/9	K	GB%	BABIP
2019	STA	A-	20	0	0	0	4	4	10^{2}	6	0	0.8	11.0	13	52%	.240
2020	*NYA*	*MLB*	*21*	*2*	*2*	*0*	*33*	*0*	*35*	*35*	*5*	*4.0*	*8.5*	*33*	*43%*	*.300*

Comparables: Tyler Alexander, Brett Cecil, Clay Buchholz

Sikkema was selected in the supplemental round of the 2019 amateur draft—an additional pick coming via the Sonny Gray trade—after dominating at Missouri to the tune of a 1.32 ERA during his junior season. He made four abbreviated appearances with Staten Island, and was thoroughly dominant by being stingy with the walks and plentiful with the grounders. The 20-year-old southpaw profiles as a likely reliever due to both his size and his non-ideal delivery, with potential to be a shutdown closer, though a future as a starter isn't completely off the table.

YEAR	TEAM	LVL	AGE	WHIP	ERA	DRA	WARP	MPH	FB%	WHF	CSP
2019	STA	A-	20	0.66	0.84	2.02	0.4				
2020	*NYA*	*MLB*	*21*	*1.45*	*4.85*	*4.94*	*0.1*				

LINEOUTS

Hitters

HITTER	POS	TEAM	LVL	AGE	PA	R	2B	3B	HR	RBI	BB	K	SB	CS	AVG/OBP/SLG	DRC+	WARP
Kevin Alcantara	CF	YAN	Rk	16	128	19	5	2	1	13	3	27	3	3	.260/.289/.358	108	0.4
Ezequiel Duran	2B	STA	A-	20	277	49	12	4	13	37	25	77	11	4	.256/.329/.496	160	3.0
Terrance Gore	OF	SWB	AAA	28	69	8	3	1	0	1	12	17	3	0	.164/.324/.255	64	-0.2
	OF	KCA	MLB	28	58	13	2	1	0	1	6	18	13	5	.275/.362/.353	68	-0.2
Zack Granite	CF	NAS	AAA	26	541	66	18	8	3	37	31	45	25	13	.290/.331/.375	76	0.5
Rosell Herrera	UT	NWO	AAA	26	180	21	11	1	5	24	14	32	2	1	.309/.367/.479	115	0.7
	UT	MIA	MLB	26	119	10	6	0	2	11	11	27	4	1	.200/.288/.314	72	-0.3
Erik Kratz	C	SFN	MLB	39	36	1	2	0	1	3	2	6	0	0	.125/.222/.281	73	0.1
	C	SWB	AAA	39	176	27	10	0	7	31	17	21	1	0	.299/.375/.500	123	1.5
	C	TBA	MLB	39	17	0	0	0	0	0	0	8	0	0	.059/.059/.059	37	-0.1
Kendrys Morales	1B	NYA	MLB	36	75	7	1	0	1	5	12	6	0	0	.177/.320/.242	83	-0.2
	1B	OAK	MLB	36	126	9	1	1	1	7	14	20	0	0	.204/.310/.259	87	-0.1
Everson Pereira	CF	STA	A-	18	74	9	3	0	1	3	4	26	3	0	.171/.216/.257	35	-0.1
Anthony Seigler	C	CSC	A	20	120	10	3	0	0	6	20	28	1	0	.175/.328/.206	73	0.2
Canaan Smith	LF	CSC	A	20	528	67	32	3	11	74	74	108	16	4	.307/.405/.465	182	5.4
Josh Smith	SS	STA	A-	21	141	17	6	1	3	15	25	17	6	3	.324/.450/.477	207	1.7

Kevin Alcantara made his stateside debut at 16 years old and brings a plus arm, plus speed and above average raw power to potential otherworldly upside, which is fitting since the week he was born, Men In Black II was the top-grossing movie in the United States. ⚾ **Ezequiel Duran** is full of potential, with no present defensive weakness and loads of raw talent. His plate approach needs some polishing, but he led the New York-Penn League in home runs and flashes impressive bat speed to make up for it. ⚾ With due respect to **Terrance Gore**, whose pinch-running prowess has been a fun October subplot over the past half-decade, you can tell it was a lost season for the Royals because they gave him 58 plate appearances. Oh, and because they sent him to the Yankees in July for cash considerations. ⚾ **Zack Granite** once hit .470 during the month of June (in 2017), encompassing 117 at-bats at Triple-A Rochester. However, that fun fact might have more staying power than the speed-and-contact lefty. ⚾ Ever bought a pair of sunglasses that looked better on the model than they did on you? **Rosell Herrera** knows how you feel. He upped his launch angle and walked more often last season, but instead of a breakout all he got was a pink slip from the Marlins. The Yankees signed Herrera in January in a move that can be described only as a heat check. ⚾ An organizational guy who provides depth and is well-liked by fans and teammates alike, **Erik Kratz**, is a solid insurance policy. There if you need him, but you silently hope you never do. ⚾ Few players in recent memory have had such Late Career A's Energy as **Kendrys Morales**, but the former slugger couldn't hack it in Oakland or New York. MLB would need to add more than just a 26th roster spot for him to stick at this point. ⚾ His offensive numbers aren't pretty and he's been knocked out of the Yankees top 20 prospects, but **Everson Pereira** still utilizes his plus speed in center. The Yankees have been aggressive with his assignments and he's plenty young enough to grow into some power. ⚾ In keeping with the trend of the Yankees season, **Anthony Seigler** spent ample time out due to injury. The young athletic catcher appeared in only 30 games throughout his first full professional season, but still showed off his plus-plus arm that pairs well with a quick release that will dominate the running game. ⚾ **Canaan Smith** is a pure hitter, with raw power and advanced barrel control. A doubles machine, he currently lacks the ability to tap into his full power potential in-game and the big parks of the Florida State League in 2020 won't help there. ⚾ When your name is **Josh Smith** you have to be really good to stand out, and a .450 on-base percentage in his pro debut allowed him to do just that.

Pitchers

PITCHER	TEAM	LVL	AGE	W	L	SV	G	GS	IP	H	HR	BB/9	K/9	K	GB%	WHIP	ERA	DRA	WARP
Albert Abreu	TRN	AA	23	5	8	0	23	20	96^2	103	9	4.9	8.5	91	43%	1.61	4.28	6.77	-2.2
Jake Barrett	SWB	AAA	27	0	1	1	10	0	15^1	10	0	2.3	11.7	20	49%	0.91	1.17	2.38	0.6
	NYA	MLB	27	0	0	0	2	0	3^2	6	2	4.9	9.8	4	8%	2.18	14.73	7.79	-0.1
Roansy Contreras	CSC	A	19	12	5	0	24	24	132^1	105	10	2.4	7.7	113	42%	1.07	3.33	3.94	1.9
Frank German	TAM	A+	21	4	4	0	16	15	76	70	9	4.1	9.7	82	46%	1.38	3.79	5.94	-0.9
Luis Gil	CSC	A	21	4	5	0	17	17	83	60	1	4.2	12.1	112	50%	1.19	2.39	3.89	1.3
	TAM	A+	21	1	0	0	3	3	13	11	0	5.5	7.6	11	40%	1.46	4.85	5.60	-0.1
Yoendrys Gomez	PUL	Rk+	19	4	2	0	6	6	29^2	26	1	3.0	8.5	28	45%	1.21	2.12	3.68	0.8
	CSC	A	19	0	3	0	6	6	26^2	28	2	3.0	8.4	25	43%	1.39	6.07	5.78	-0.2
Ben Heller	SWB	AAA	27	0	0	1	9	4	11	5	0	2.5	10.6	13	55%	0.73	0.82	1.77	0.5
	NYA	MLB	27	0	0	0	6	0	7^1	6	1	3.7	11.0	9	50%	1.23	1.23	5.06	0.0
Mike King	TRN	AA	24	0	1	0	3	2	12^2	20	1	1.4	5.7	8	51%	1.74	9.95	6.92	-0.3
	SWB	AAA	24	3	1	0	4	3	23^2	20	3	2.3	10.6	28	48%	1.10	4.18	2.99	0.8
	NYA	MLB	24	0	0	0	1	0	2	2	0	0.0	4.5	1	38%	1.00	0.00	5.19	0.0
Brooks Kriske	TAM	A+	25	1	1	1	7	0	12	4	0	3.8	12.0	16	43%	0.75	0.00	2.61	0.3
	TRN	AA	25	2	2	11	36	0	48^2	30	3	4.3	11.8	64	32%	1.09	2.59	3.88	0.4
Brady Lail	TRN	AA	25	3	1	1	14	1	31	18	1	3.5	13.6	47	45%	0.97	1.74	2.73	0.7
	SWB	AAA	25	1	1	0	11	0	15^2	19	3	1.7	9.8	17	40%	1.40	7.47	4.91	0.2
	NYA	MLB	25	0	0	0	1	0	2^2	2	1	3.4	6.8	2	57%	1.12	10.12	6.01	0.0
Jonathan Loaisiga	SWB	AAA	24	0	2	0	5	4	15^2	14	3	2.9	10.9	19	49%	1.21	6.32	3.20	0.5
	NYA	MLB	24	2	2	0	15	4	31^2	31	6	4.5	10.5	37	40%	1.48	4.55	5.33	0.1
Tyler Lyons	IND	AAA	31	4	3	3	35	0	45^2	34	4	3.2	10.8	55	40%	1.09	3.35	3.31	1.3
	PIT	MLB	31	1	1	0	3	0	4	6	1	6.8	11.2	5	33%	2.25	11.25	5.17	0.0
	NYA	MLB	31	0	1	0	11	0	8^2	7	3	2.1	12.5	12	32%	1.04	4.15	4.91	0.0
Luis Medina	CSC	A	20	1	8	0	20	20	93	86	9	6.5	11.1	115	47%	1.65	6.00	7.09	-2.1
	TAM	A+	20	0	0	0	2	2	10^2	7	0	2.5	10.1	12	71%	0.94	0.84	3.52	0.2
Nick Nelson	TRN	AA	23	7	2	0	13	12	65	48	4	4.8	11.5	83	31%	1.28	2.35	4.62	0.3
	SWB	AAA	23	1	1	0	4	4	21	20	2	3.0	10.3	24	45%	1.29	4.71	2.75	0.8
Clarke Schmidt	TAM	A+	23	4	5	0	13	12	63^1	59	2	3.4	9.8	69	57%	1.31	3.84	4.13	0.7
	TRN	AA	23	2	0	0	3	3	19	14	1	0.5	9.0	19	45%	0.79	2.37	3.84	0.3
Stephen Tarpley	SWB	AAA	26	5	1	3	18	2	31^2	25	3	3.7	9.7	34	66%	1.20	3.13	2.90	1.0
	NYA	MLB	26	1	0	2	21	1	24^2	34	6	5.5	12.4	34	36%	1.99	6.93	4.15	0.3
Nick Tropeano	SLC	AAA	28	4	6	0	17	15	79^2	90	12	3.5	9.6	85	36%	1.52	5.87	4.25	1.9
	LAA	MLB	28	0	1	0	3	1	13^2	18	6	4.0	6.6	10	25%	1.76	9.88	9.14	-0.5
Miguel Yajure	TAM	A+	21	8	6	0	22	18	127^2	110	5	2.0	8.6	122	55%	1.08	2.26	3.82	1.8
	TRN	AA	21	1	0	0	2	2	11	9	0	1.6	9.0	11	36%	1.00	0.82	5.08	0.0

Albert Abreu still comes with quite a bit of risk. And while questions of his long-term durability and a history of injuries cast a shadow, a fastball that can scrape 99 makes him more than worth it. ⚾ **Jake Barrett** gave up five runs to the Mariners in one of his two major-league appearances of the season. There's no joke here. How do you give up five runs to the Mariners? ⚾ Currently on track to become a mid-rotation/back-end starter, **Roansy Contreras** is another Yankee arm already flashing major-league level stuff, but durability is the biggest question mark given his frame. ⚾ **Frank German** wields a mid-90's fastball alongside a pair of solid secondary offerings. Sound familiar? The Yankees are practically creating these guys from thin air and hoarding them. ⚾ **Luis Gil** is a big strikeout guy. His fastball sits at 95-97 mph from a seemingly effortless delivery, but his other pitches aren't quite there yet largely due to lack of command. ⚾ At 6-foot-3, 175 pounds with room to add onto the frame, **Yoendrys Gomez**'s physical presence on the mound is a daunting one, as is his rapidly improving changeup. ⚾ **Ben Heller** worked his way back from Tommy John surgery in September and even got to be on the postseason roster for a few days after he replaced CC Sabathia on the ALCS roster when he went down. ⚾ **Michael King** has a fairly impressive mix of average pitches in his arsenal. A four-seamer, cutter, change and slider all play second fiddle to his best offering: a sinker. King could be a back-end starter, but his best hope is to get close to Zack Britton and pick his brain. ⚾ **Brooks Kriske** entered 2019 as an afterthought, a senior sign reliever from 2016 that hadn't pitched much as a pro due to ill-timed Tommy John surgery. After a season of minors dominance off a fastball up to 98 MPH, a plus slider and an interesting new splitter, he exited it as a 40-man roster member and real prospect. ⚾ In his major-league debut, **Brady Lail** recorded his first strikeout with his family excitedly cheering him on from the stands. He was immediately sent back down to Triple-A following the outing, never to return. ⚾ Former top prospect **Jonathan Loaisiga** didn't seem nearly as sharp or promising this season. The stuff is there as he flirted with triple digits, but location is everything and neither his current level of command nor his inability to stay healthy will separate him in a system full of ripe, young arms. ⚾ **Luis Medina** has all the raw stuff of a future star—a plus-plus fastball that frequents 98, and two plus off-speed pitches to go along with it—none of which will matter if he can't throw them for strikes. ⚾ **Nick Nelson**'s high-quality curve is both a set-up and putaway pitch, his mid-90's fastball garners swings and misses with late life and his changeup and slider are each solid enough to round out his repertoire. ⚾ While it's likely he ends up as a reliever, **Clarke Schmidt** is slowly but surely working up to his full potential. His strikeout numbers are impressive, and pitched into the seventh inning in three of his last four starts; not too shabby for his first season of work after Tommy John surgery. ⚾ **Stephen Tarpley** is just a LOOGY in a world where they're becoming obsolete and righties have anagrammed his name into El Party via a career .378/.474/.634 line against him. ⚾ In another era and with different elbow ligaments, **Nick Tropeano** might have been something. As it is, both his pre- and post-TJ selves gave up a few too many walks, and way too many fly balls. In 2019, these traits led, first, to Salt Lake City, and ultimately, out of the organization altogether. ⑱ **Miguel Yajure** has flown under the radar in a Yankees system deep with pitching of all sorts, but he's a potential future rotation piece, now up to the mid-90s with command and good feel for a changeup. He was protected from Rule 5 despite a crowded 40-man situation.

Yankees Prospects

The State of the System

It's your typical Yankees system. They have arms that jumped in Double-A, arms that will jump sometime in the next two years in Double-A, and Estevan Florial again.

The Top Ten

★ ★ ★ *2020 Top 101 Prospect* **#24** ★ ★ ★

1 **Deivi Garcia** **RHP** OFP: 70 ETA: mid 2020
Born: 05/19/99 Age: 21 Bats: R Throws: R Height: 5'9" Weight: 163
Origin: International Free Agent, 2015

The Report: Start with a deceptive fastball that he can get regularly into the mid 90s. Add a plus-plus curveball. Sprinkle in an average change that flashes higher. Stir with a plus slider…wait, Deivi García has a plus slider now?

A lot of things came together in 2019. García threw 111 1/3 innings, setting a new career high by over 35 and reducing concerns that he might end up in relief because of his slight frame and low innings counts in the low-minors. His velocity bumped up a little. His curveball command tightened. His changeup consistency improved. He got an awful lot of swings and misses from high-minors hitters. He nearly earned a September call-up from a pennant contender. He did it all during a year in which he didn't turn 20 until a month-and-a-half into the season.

The addition of a slider during the season is the most intriguing development in 2019 for his future profile, and it was a plus pitch for him almost immediately. Nick Stellini spoke to García about the emergence of the pitch this past summer. In short, it's a key addition to an arsenal that now looks a lot more like an upper-rotation starter than it did at this time last year.

Variance: Medium. There's relief risk due to his size and inconsistent command, but he's pretty close to MLB-ready and inched closer to a full workload this season.

Ben Carsley's Fantasy Take: Concerns about size be damned; García is a fantasy stud in the making. It'd be nice if he were headed for greener pitching pastures than Yankee Stadium, to be sure, but he should pile up wins and strikeouts in pinstripes. Plus, as discussed above, he's pretty much ready now.

It's possible that the Yankees don't call him up until mid-season and use him in more of a spot-start or hybrid role, but I think by early 2021, at the latest, we'll have a bona fide fantasy SP3 with upside here. Buy, buy, buy.

★ ★ ★ *2020 Top 101 Prospect* **#46** ★ ★ ★

2 **Jasson Dominguez OF** OFP: 70 ETA: 2023-2026
Born: 02/07/03 Age: 17 Bats: B Throws: R Height: 5'10" Weight: 190
Origin: International Free Agent, 2019

The Report: The primary basis for our list products is our own in-person staff looks. We don't have staff looks at *every* player on every list, although we strive to and came pretty close this year. We supplement that with background discussion with a fairly large network of industry sources—primarily pro scouts who base *their* opinions on *their* in-person looks.

This presents a recurring problem for players who have yet to make their stateside debut. Much to my eternal dismay, we don't have live staff coverage in the Dominican Republic at the moment. Teams are starting to scout the DSL and the informal Tricky League instructs more than they used to, but their coverage is incomplete. Therefore, our access to scout opinions out of there is a lot more uneven than it is for any level of stateside baseball. And, of course, many of the highest-profile J2 signees have been hidden from sight for some time before signing because they agreed to illegal early deals, so the period in which they're available to opposing scouts after being signed is short.

Jasson Dominguez has yet to make his pro debut. We know a lot about him anyway. He's one of the highest-profile J2 signees ever, a potential five-tool center fielder touted as the next Mike Trout or Mickey Mantle. The Yankees made an early deal for him and blew their entire pool to do it. He did play in the Tricky League and fall instructs this summer, and reviews were universally positive.

It would be a silly exercise to omit Dominguez from this list. He's obviously one of the best prospects in this system. There was some early internal support for him to make the 101, and we ultimately placed him in the top 50. But we have live looks at all 21 other players on this list, plus the ability to get industry reports backchecking them. We *don't* have that for Dominguez, and all we'd be doing writing a scouting report on him is repeating low-confidence second/third-hand information about a 16-year-old that hasn't yet made his pro debut.

Variance: Extreme. Kevin Maitan was the last J2 to make the 101 the following offseason.

Ben Carsley's Fantasy Take: Were dynasty baseball an endeavor for sane people, guys like Dominguez would not be valued quite so highly out of the chute. Sure, there's a chance that he's the next Ronald Acuña Jr., but there's also a chance that he's the next [INSERT FAILED J2 PROSPECT HERE]. Despite the insane volatility, the prospect of a franchise-changing player is just too alluring for most, and guys like Dominguez end up being valued way more than immediate contributors with lower ceilings. Essentially, I *wish* that I could say it's a year too early to buy in on Dominguez. But the reality is this: if you don't buy now, you'll never get the chance. It's up to you if you want to take on the risk/eat the roster spot for a half-decade, but the upside is certainly there.

3 **Albert Abreu RHP** OFP: 60 ETA: 2020
Born: 09/26/95 Age: 24 Bats: R Throws: R Height: 6'2" Weight: 175
Origin: International Free Agent, 2013

The Report: Abreu bounced back from an injury-marred 2017 and 2018 to have a, uh, slightly less injury-marred 2019. Look, when he's on the mound and right, the stuff is electric. Abreu features an explosive high-90s fastball that touched 99 for me and has reportedly hit triple digits. It's a high-spin pitch with late life up in the zone, and he can change eye levels with it despite only average overall command due to some weird timing stuff in his delivery. It's a plus-plus fastball as a starter, and it's not impossible that the heater could be a true 8 out of the pen. His curveball is an easy plus projection, a power breaker that he can manipulate, and he shows better command of the breaking ball than the fastball. Like most Yankees pitching prospects in the upper minors, Abreu has added a slider. Although it flashes, it is well behind his curveball at present. The change is also fringy. It's firm and he can struggle to turn it over at times, but the pitch has flashed more than changeups normally do for pitchers with his profile. Abreu ultimately possesses the ingredients to start, if both his command and his right arm cooperate over the long term.

Variance: High. Abreu has thrown 100 innings only once in a season, and that happened back in 2016. This year it was a bicep issue that sidelined him for a bit—another injury that just adds to the worrying cornucopia of arm issues that have plagued him over the years. If you were confident that he could take the ball 30 times a year, the overall profile is only a whisker off Deivi. We're not that confident, so he's here.

Ben Carsley's Fantasy Take: The Yankees sure do have a lot of dudes with this fantasy profile! Standard caveats about investing in fantasy pitchers aside, there's a lot to like about Abreu, who has insane strikeout upside and who is very close to the majors. That being said, there are a few scenarios that one can envision in which Abreu's fantasy production won't match his stuff. The Yankees could use him in a quasi-opener role as they attempt to build up his innings, preventing him from earning wins. Likewise, Abreu could end up serving as a non-closing, high-leverage relief arm that's only usable in the very deepest of leagues. The uncertainty about his future role knocks his top-50-type talent down to a likely back-of-the-top-101 ranking for me.

4 **Luis Medina RHP** OFP: 60 ETA: 2022
Born: 05/03/99 Age: 21 Bats: R Throws: R Height: 6'1" Weight: 175
Origin: International Free Agent, 2015

The Report: Medina began this year as he had in most others—wowing sparse crowds with radar-gun readings that touched triple digits while walking well over a batter an inning. The overall stat line for the season isn't great. It suffers from too many free passes from when he couldn't find the zone, as well as hard contact from when he found too much of it. Something seemed to click around early July, though, when he began a dominant run that resulted in a late-August promotion to Tampa, something that didn't seem likely back in April and May. Medina went at least five innings in each of his final six Sally League starts, allowing three or more runs only once and never striking out fewer than seven. He posted double-digit strikeouts three times in that stretch.

Medina's stuff has always been great, beginning, of course, with an upper-90s fastball that has both late life and plane. It is especially effective up and above the zone. Less talked about are the two secondaries, both of which regularly flash plus. His low- to mid-80s curve has a couple different looks to it. It can be 11-5 with strong vertical action on the lower end, while being more of a power slurve at the upper. Both variations show good, late bite.

His high-80s change is advanced, given the overall stage of his development, and it features convincing arm speed and real fade. Medina is athletic, and his frame is filling out nicely. He also looks taller than his listed height. If you want to nitpick, his delivery could be more fluid, but the control and command seem to be improving as he grows into his body. Next year will be an important one for Medina. He will try to consolidate the gains he has made with his control, while continuing to refine his command, as he works toward the realization of his plus potential.

Variance: High, and this works in both directions. It is possible that the recent gains in control regress, and the command doesn't get to where it needs to be, which pushes him to the pen. It is also possible that Medina really has flipped a switch, and the stuff could be top-of-the-rotation level.

Ben Carsley's Fantasy Take: The Yankees sure do have a lot of dudes with this fantasy profile! While Abreu may have slightly higher upside and a better ETA, I actually prefer Medina, who I think has a better shot to start long-term. He's already owned in deeper dynasty leagues, of course, but if you play in a shallower one, you'll need to buy now. As soon as his 2019 improvements prove to be real, he will skyrocket up the rankings. Whenever I make dynasty top-101 predictions this early in the process, I tend to regret it, but I think he should make our upcoming edition of the list.

5 **Luis Gil** **RHP** OFP: 55 ETA: 2022
Born: 06/03/98 Age: 22 Bats: R Throws: R Height: 6'3" Weight: 176
Origin: International Free Agent, 2015

The Report: Traded to the Yankees from the Twins in 2018, Gil has quickly made a name for himself within the organization. He features a dominant fastball-curveball combination that helped him strike out 123 batters in 96 innings between both A-ball levels. His 95-98 mph fastball is a plus one. It has ride and is also aided by Gil's ability to create downhill plane. The delivery was effortless, suggesting that he may be able to add a tick with further physical growth. But the fastball is already a swing-and-miss pitch.

Gil's best secondary offering is an 81-84 slurvy curveball that has sweeping action and plus depth. Although the command of this pitch can waver, the shape stays steady, and it's his go-to out pitch. His third pitch is a 90-92 mph power changeup. It's fairly new for Gil, which is evident because it still lacks movement or even average command. His biggest issue is consistency. He can be erratic and lose the strike zone at times. He also has a tendency to overthrow his fastball, especially when behind in the count. Despite the control issues, Gil has potentially high-end stuff and intriguing upside.

Variance: High. Throwing strikes and repeating his delivery remain concerns for the 21-year-old. There is also a chance that he will wind up as a high-leverage reliever instead of a starter, if he can't develop a third pitch.

Ben Carsley's Fantasy Take: The Yankees sure do have a lot of dudes with this fantasy profile! He's my least-favorite arm among the Abreu/Medina/Gil trio, yet Gil still has a reasonable argument to rank among the top-150-or-so dynasty prospects. If you feel as though you have a solid grasp of which of these three arms is gonna end up in the rotation versus the bullpen, please let us know, because to be honest it's anyone's guess right now.

6 **Anthony Volpe SS** OFP: 55 ETA: 2023

Born: 04/28/01 Age: 19 Bats: R Throws: R Height: 5'11" Weight: 180
Origin: Round 1, 2019 Draft (#30 overall)

The Report: Volpe doesn't exactly fit the mold of your traditional first-round prep shortstop. The tools don't really pop like they do with Bobby Witt or CJ Abrams, but he's a very well-rounded player with a decent shot to stick at short. He's more polished than quick-twitch at the six, too, with solid hands, solid actions, and enough arm for the left side. He'd be an asset defensively if he had to slide to second or third.

He looks the part at the plate as well. His hands and hips work well, helping to generate above-average bat speed. His sturdy frame stays balanced throughout the swing, although he can get a little wrap at times, which adds length to the bat path. The swing is fairly flat at present, and there's minimal physical projection left in his frame, so the ultimate power ceiling remains an open question. He's a strong kid, though, so I wouldn't be shocked if he unlocks average game power with a bit more lift.

Volpe offers a broad base of skills, but you'd struggle to find anything higher than a 55 on the scouting sheet. Sometimes those profiles play up, but if one of the offensive tools—or the shortstop glove—fall short of projection, it's a quick slide from above-average regular to bench piece.

Variance: High. He's more polished than your usual prep shortstop, but he's just as far away and no less risky.

Ben Carsley's Fantasy Take: Volpe reads as more well-rounded than special, and while the potential shortstop eligibility is intriguing, not much in the rest of the package is. He could sneak onto the back of some top-101 lists once he's much closer to the majors, but at three-plus seasons out, the relative lack of upside doesn't justify a heavy dynasty investment at this point. Between being a Yankee and a first-rounder, he's likely to be overvalued.

7

Estevan Florial OF OFP: 55 ETA: 2021
Born: 11/25/97 Age: 22 Bats: L Throws: R Height: 6'1" Weight: 185
Origin: International Free Agent, 2015

The Report: Florial made his unofficial Double-A debut in the 2017 Eastern League playoffs, capping off a season in which he rose from toolsy sleeper to top outfield prospect. We expected him to spend most of 2018 for real at Double-A and even projected 2019 as his major-league ETA. The stats above will tell you that not only did he not make his major-league debut in 2019, but also that he spent the entire season in the Florida State League and struggled all the while. What on earth happened?

A series of hand and wrist injuries is a good place to start. Florial has missed nearly half a year in each of the last two seasons, with the bulk of that time coming from two breaks in his right hamate area. Hamate injuries are notorious for sapping hitting ability, especially power, for some time after the player returns to action. That's a partial explanation for Florial's offensive struggles over the past two years, but he has also just not mastered pitching in the way that we had hoped two years ago. His approach simply has never improved much.

We aren't entirely getting off the bandwagon here. He still has outstanding underlying tools: the bat speed, the raw power, and the overall athleticism. We're just becoming less sure of the hit-tool development as each year passes where we don't see it.

Variance: High. He needs to get it going, but there's significant upside beyond the OFP if the tools finally click.

Ben Carsley's Fantasy Take: I'm mad at Florial. He made me love him, and he's given me nothing in return. I understand that the tools remain, and you're not at all crazy if you value him as a top-101 prospect still. Personally, I don't. Perhaps I'm just being a spiteful ex-lover, but I don't think Florial is worth the risk now that we understand the ceiling is lower.

8 **Ezequiel Duran 2B** OFP: 55 ETA: Late 2022
Born: 05/22/99 Age: 21 Bats: R Throws: R Height: 5'11" Weight: 185
Origin: International Free Agent, 2017

The Report: I wrote an entire column earlier this year about my decision to stuff Ezequiel Duran, so it should be no surprise that he ended up highly-ranked even in a very deep Yankees system. Most important is the combination of plus raw power and a potential plus glove at second. Duran has above-average bat speed with loft. He can cover major-league-quality velocity, turning on it inside and using the big part of the park when it's away. I wasn't sure, at the time, how quickly it would play in games because he liked to drive the gaps, but then he went and led the Penn League in home runs, so…

In the infield, he's a polished, rangy fielder, with good hands and actions. He probably doesn't have quite enough range or arm to slide over to short in non-emergency situations, but the arm and range are both above-average for the keystone. He's a smooth defender, and there's no weakness. I know we don't usually gush about second-base defense, but he's fun to watch in a Robinson Canó kind of way.

The overall approach at the plate is still a little raw. You could lock him up front door with breaking balls, and he'd expand up more than you'd like for fastballs. Both of those are fixable with reps, but given the grip-it-and-rip-it style, I can't project more than an average hit tool at present. That should be enough to get the power into games and make him a nice everyday guy at second. There's more in the tank here, too, as he doesn't have a ton of pro reps and was banged up for much of 2018.

Variance: High. He has no full-season track record, and it might be a fringe hit tool if he doesn't make adjustments to his approach (specifically spin). He might grow off the middle infield, but I suspect we are going to be less concerned about that than other sources. He also might be a Top 101 guy next year with a good campaign in Charleston (and not a back-end guy).

Ben Carsley's Fantasy Take: Anyone else getting a Jonathan Schoop vibe from that report? There's plenty of value in a guy like Schoop in deeper leagues, of course, but not so much that you'd want to roster the prospect version of him unless your league stored roughly 200 minor leaguers. Duran is an interesting add, for sure, but don't get too carried away.

9 **Clarke Schmidt RHP** OFP: 50 ETA: 2020/21
Born: 02/20/96 Age: 24 Bats: R Throws: R Height: 6'1" Weight: 200
Origin: Round 1, 2017 Draft (#16 overall)

The Report: In his first full year back on the field since his 2017 Tommy John surgery, Schmidt showed the power stuff that made him a first-round pick. He offers a mid-90s fastball that is an above-average offering, a plus slider, and a solid frame. Schmidt did miss time this year with the flu and with right forearm soreness that kept him out of action for nearly a month. The changeup isn't great, more of a show-me pitch that he telegraphs, and the overall fastball command leaves a lot to be desired. Given these concerns, it is more likely that he ends up in the bullpen long term.

Variance: Medium. The stuff is good no matter the role, but the injury history is cause for concern.

Ben Carsley's Fantasy Take: Nah. The upside isn't high enough, and in an organization this loaded with pitching talent, it's tough to see how Schmidt remains a long-term starter anyway. You can pass.

10 **Kevin Alcantara OF** OFP: 55 ETA: 2023
Born: 07/12/02 Age: 17 Bats: R Throws: R Height: 6'6" Weight: 188
Origin: International Free Agent, 2018

The Report: Alcantara oozes projection. He played half the season at 16 years old, turning 17 in July. It looks like he could add 30-plus pounds of good weight, which makes the profile even more exciting, given his current tool set. He has plus speed, present above-average raw power, and plus arm strength. He could grow into even more power as he matures and will most likely not face a pitcher younger than him until he is 18 years old. In the outfield he tracks balls well with long graceful strides, but he might have to settle into a corner spot as his body matures and he loses a step or two. He struggled against better velocity and offspeed stuff simply because he has never seen it before. There is boom-or-bust potential, but the boom would require industrial-strength ear protection.

Variance: Is there a grade higher than Extreme? He is very young and didn't light the world on fire in his stateside debut. There is a wide range of outcomes.

Ben Carsley's Fantasy Take: If you enjoyed betting on Florial, you'll love the sequel in Alcantara: 2 Fast 2 Florial. That's not entirely fair, of course—they're different players despite the similarities in skill sets—but you can treat Florial's trials as a cautionary tale of sorts as to what might happen with Alcantara. Still, we can't fully ignore his upside. If you're filling out the bottom of your roster in a TDGX-sized (200-plus prospects rostered) league, it's reasonable to gamble on Alcantara.

The Next Ten

11 **Roansy Contreras RHP**
Born: 11/07/99 Age: 20 Bats: R Throws: R Height: 6'0" Weight: 175
Origin: International Free Agent, 2016

He's a small pitcher in the Deivi García mold rather than the power builds of Luises Gil and Medina, and Contreras does not have their explosiveness or upside of any of those three. Even so, he shouldn't go unmentioned in a discussion about the Yanks' collection of young arms. Listed six-foot and 175 pounds, the

Dominican righty is athletic with a smooth enough delivery to project above-average command. Contreras is mainly a two-pitch guy at present, with a fastball sitting low-to-mid 90s that has touched 96. This is an above-average pitch that could be plus with command refinement, as it features some late life and run.

His most intriguing offering is his curve, which shows tight 11-5 shape and finishes with late and sharp break. He can throw it for strikes but wastes it in the dirt too much at present. Still, this should be a future plus pitch. His upper-80s change comes in pretty firm and is a distant third in the present arsenal, but it flashes some dive and fade and could become at least average in time. After performing very well as a teenager in the Sally League, Contreras will hit High-A Tampa in 2020.

12 **Yoendrys Gomez RHP**

Born: 10/15/99 Age: 20 Bats: R Throws: R Height: 6'3" Weight: 175
Origin: International Free Agent, 2016

Gomez has slowly grown on me from a good org arm to a nice developmental project to one of the next good major league arms they'll churn out of this organization. He's grown into his lanky body and now fires plus fastballs which are tough to square up when he's spotting it up in the zone. Gomez can tend to overthrow his pitches and miss spots, which doesn't allow the fastball to play as high as the velocity grade at present. He pairs the heater with a potential plus changeup and average curveball. The *cambio* is his go-to pitch, as it has late split-finger-like action and can generate a fair amount of weak contact. The curve is inconsistent. It can get slurvy and roll into the zone, or be vulnerable to hard contact when it rides up. Next season could be a breakout year for Gomez, and he might be in the mix with the top arms in the system on our 2021 list.

13 **Michael King RHP**

Born: 05/25/95 Age: 25 Bats: R Throws: R Height: 6'3" Weight: 210
Origin: Round 12, 2016 Draft (#353 overall)

It was a weird season for King. He was one of the "shut down in February with vague elbow problems while ramping up" guys from this spring. He wouldn't show up on the mound until July, and didn't get stretched out until August, so it was an extremely abbreviated MiLB season for him. We got a bunch of staff looks on him, and his velocity was varied wildly from start-to-start, but at times he was the 91-93 mph sinkerballer with plus command from 2018 that projected as a mid-rotation starter. He was then a very delayed September call-up for emergency innings, and got into one relief outing in late September, where he pitched well. King mixes in a four-seam, change, slider, and cutter with the sinker, but none of them currently project as above-average; it's the sinker that's going to make or break his career. We are concerned about the durability now given a five month elbow-injury-wrecked his season, but a No. 3/4 innings-eater type starting outcome is still quite plausible here. A ground-ball specialist out of the pen isn't a bad fallback.

14 **T.J. Sikkema LHP**
Born: 07/25/98 Age: 21 Bats: L Throws: L Height: 6'0" Weight: 221
Origin: Round 1, 2019 Draft (#38 overall)

A polished Mizzou arm who had a career 2.38 ERA in the SEC as well as a 1.72 ERA on the Cape, Sikkema wasn't talked about as much as other top arms in that conference. It isn't for a lack of stuff, though, as his fastball is up to 95 from a variety of angles and he features a deceptive crossfire delivery. The breaking balls all flash above-average, and come in from a variety of angles. There's a potentially average changeup as well. Sikkema might have gotten overlooked because he doesn't have an ideal frame—it's a thick, barrel chested, 6-foot-even—and the delivery isn't ideal either given the crossfire and angle. But sometimes the results speak for themselves, and in a system known for developing arms this is an arm that can jump.

15 **Frank German LHP**
Born: 09/22/97 Age: 22 Bats: R Throws: R Height: 6'2" Weight: 195
Origin: Round 4, 2018 Draft (#127 overall)

One of the Yankees favorite types of draft pick—a day two, Directional Florida arm—German dealt with elbow soreness late in spring, and a shoulder strain which cost him the month of July. We already had reliever concerns here, and the 2019 durability issues won't do much to assuage those. When he was on the mound, though, German maintained his velocity gains from 2018, pumping mid-90s heat and pairing the fastball with a pair of potentially average secondaries. The arsenal and the frame is a starting pitcher, but we've still never seen him stretched out as a pro, so he more or less holds serve within the Yankees system. But as we have to write for basically every arm in this range, German is a guy who could jump in 2020. And all he really has to do is stay healthy.

16 **Antonio Cabello RHP**
Born: 11/01/00 Age: 19 Bats: R Throws: R Height: 5'10" Weight: 160
Origin: International Free Agent, 2017

It was a year to forget for Cabello, who has struggled to show the same loud tools since dislocating his shoulder in late 2018. Last year this was an all-star profile—a potential plus hitter with plus speed and arm strength who profiled well in center field. Since the injury Cabello has looked lost at the plate, flailing at pitches and not driving the ball with the same authority he showed in the complex. He has also lost a step out on the grass, moving him to a corner outfield spot. He is still young—he spent the whole season at age 18—so you hope that with more time away from his injury the tools can come back.

17 **Anthony Seigler** C

Born: 06/20/99 Age: 21 Bats: B Throws: S Height: 6'0" Weight: 200
Origin: Round 1, 2018 Draft (#23 overall)

Last year's first-rounder had a lost season in his first full year of pro ball. He debuted for the River Dogs in mid-June following a quad strain and 30 games later was done for the season after suffering a patella fracture. Seigler didn't show much offensively during his brief stint on the field, though his approach was very solid and he drew his fair share of walks. The first impression is of a mature hitter with an opposite-field mindset and an eye towards contact, though upon further examination this gives way to concern about a somewhat timid hitter who currently struggles to drive the ball. He is slight of frame and not very projectible, which won't alleviate concerns about his future power output. Still, Seigler just turned twenty and should get a fresh shot at the level next spring.

It is a completely different story defensively, where the Georgia prep's athleticism is obvious watching him move around behind the plate. His better-than-plus arm stands out more than anything, and while he has a quick pop and release he doesn't always need it—I saw him casually gun down a runner from his knees. How he performs next year when fully healthy will say a lot about his trajectory as a prospect.

18 **Josh Stowers** OF

Born: 02/25/97 Age: 23 Bats: R Throws: R Height: 6'0" Weight: 200
Origin: Round 2, 2018 Draft (#54 overall)

Shed Long was acquired for Sonny Gray and spent about thirty seconds in the Yankees organization before he was flipped to Seattle for Stowers, a 2018 second-round pick whom New York had reportedly been high on prior to the draft. The 22-year-old outfielder flashed some tools this year in Low-A, though the overall profile sends mixed messages. Stowers is athletic, but a bit brawnier than one might expect of someone who took a third of his reps in center field. His speed is comfortably above-average but not plus, although his range in the field plays up due to his instincts and flair. He has a quick bat and a good approach but there's some swing-and-miss. He's shown some over-the-fence power, but it is more gap-to-gap at present, and there's not a lot of room for projection here. Stowers's path to the majors could take a couple different routes: he could find a way to tap into some more pop and make his way as a corner bat, or he could prove his wares in center and try to hit his way into a fourth-outfielder outcome. He'll likely start next season in High-A and could move quickly if warranted, but for now it's a tweener profile.

19 **Josh Smith SS**
Born: 08/07/97 Age: 22 Bats: L Throws: R Height: 5'10" Weight: 172
Origin: Round 2, 2019 Draft (#67 overall)

The Yankees seem to have a lot of middle infield prospects who can make contact, draw walks and play good defense. The lefty-hitting, 5-foot-10 Smith is no exception. He was one of the most patient hitters in the New York-Penn League, as evidenced by his 17 percent walk rate. He complemented this with impressive bat-to-ball skills, as well as a knack for elevating the ball at a somewhat surprising rate, especially to the pull side. The power is more gap-to-gap, though, and it's most likely going to stay that way thanks to his already maxed-out frame and average bat speed. With good range and hands but a questionable arm, his best defensive fit is at second, but he could play anywhere on the diamond in a pinch. Greg Garcia is the major league comp here, as Smith is a tweener with some attractive offensive characteristics and sufficient defensive versatility.

20 **Alexander Vizcaino RHP**
Born: 05/22/97 Age: 23 Bats: R Throws: R Height: 6'2" Weight: 160
Origin: International Free Agent, 2016

Compared to his fellow young Dominican arms–Luis Medina, Roansy Contreas and Luis Gil–Vizcaino doesn't have the same hullabaloo surrounding him. Still, he has nearly as much upside as the others. His pitchability and sequencing are impressive with his three-pitch arsenal. His fastball sits mid 90s and features arm-side tail. Command for this pitch can be lacking, but it played as an above-average pitch when thrown in the zone. Vizcaino's 88-90 mph power changeup is by far his best offering. The arm action doesn't slow down, making it a true swing-and-miss pitch, especially paired with his fastball. Displaying hard downward action and late tail, he is able to throw it to both right- and left-handed batters with success. Vizcaino's third offering is an 80-83 mph slider that lacks consistency. When he is able to snap off a good one it shows plus tilt with late bite. But feel for this pitch is still a work in progress. Due to his high-waisted, long-levered physicality, and a similar arsenal, Vizcaino reminds me a lot of Domingo German. There are no mechanical concerns, just the ability to throw strikes consistently.

Personal Cheeseball

PC **Nick Nelson RHP**
Born: 12/05/95 Age: 24 Bats: R Throws: R Height: 6'1" Weight: 195
Origin: Round 4, 2016 Draft (#128 overall)

Jarrett and Jeffrey giggled when I jokingly ("jokingly" – j.p) clamored for Nelson to be in the Yankees Top 10. I knew that wasn't going to happen, but it got the point across: I was impressed by Nelson. Set to be a Rule 5 Draft-eligible prospect this offseason, the firm-bodied righty has three average or better pitches in his fastball, curve and change. The fastball was mid-90s, touching 97 in my look, and he maintained it throughout the entire start. The curve had really nice shape, going 11-5 and getting whiffs consistently. He left some of them in the middle of the zone, but the command of the pitch improved as the game progressed. The change was less impressive, as it was a little firm. It occasionally flashed impressive tumble, though, and I'm confident there's further projection for the pitch. Nelson's age, inconsistent feel for the change and command profile would suggest he's a future reliever, but he's also relatively new to pitching and has made strides on the mound every year. He has a major league future of some sort coming—perhaps I'm the lone advocate on the staff in thinking there's a potential mid-to-backend starter—and Nelson's three pitch mix shouldn't go unnoticed.

Low Minors Sleeper

LMS **Anderson Munoz RHP**
Born: 08/04/98 Age: 21 Bats: R Throws: R Height: 5'8" Weight: 158
Origin: International Free Agent, 2017

Like Deivi Garcia, Munoz is an undersized righty with plus arm strength. His fastball sits in the low-to-mid 90s and has gotten up to 99 as a starter. He has a hard slider that lacks consistent shape and acts more like a cutter at times but will flash average with good tilt. He also has a change that serves as a change-of-pace pitch but not much else, although it's better than the average changeup you will see in the Penn League. I like Munoz because he has a very repeatable delivery and has made significant strides in his strike-throwing ability (6.44 BB/9 in 2018 vs. 3.32 in 2019 NYPL). There is a fair bit of reliever risk because of the frame and mediocre secondaries, but he's made enough strides in key areas where we're at least keeping our eyes on him.

Top Talents 25 and Under (as of 4/1/2020)

1. Gleyber Torres
2. Deivi Garcia
3. Miguel Andujar
4. Clint Frazier
5. Jasson Dominguez
6. Albert Abreu
7. Luis Medina
8. Luis Gil
9. Anthony Volpe

10. Estevan Florial

Gleyber Torres is a star. He took a small step forward with the bat, as more of his raw power started to play in games—the baseballs probably didn't hurt there either—and he was top-five in DRC+ for a second baseman. He can pitch in at shortstop adequately as well, as he did during Didi Gregorius's absence, and he still has two more years of eligibility for this 25U list. He's the overwhelming favorite to be number one in 2021 and 2022 as well and the best may be yet to come.

Garcia has the best outside shot to unseat him. If it all comes together as a front-of-the-rotation starter, he'll have a case, but Torres is already approaching his OFP 70 projection as a prospect. Garcia still has a ways to go. Andujar lost the season to a right labrum injury that eventually required surgery. He was already likely to slide across the infield, and this might accelerate the process. After his strong rookie campaign with the bat in 2018 he's likely to have a spot waiting for him, though, unlike Clint Frazier. Frazier was fine at the plate in 2019, but had some high profile defensive miscues and equally high profile spats with the notoriously easygoing NYC baseball media. He's a prime change of scenery candidate for playing time if nothing else, although he looks more like an average regular in a corner nowadays than a future star.

Tyler Wade is a useful super-utility type on a team a bit worse than the Yankees, although the hit tool never developed as well as we'd hoped against major league arms. Chance Adams has struggled to regain his velocity or command after arm issues. Pitchers, man. The Yankees have graduated a lot of top prospect talent in recent seasons, much of which currently forms the core of their 100-win division winner. It's still a strong system overall, but there's less immediate help on the farm and some uncertainty with the Andujars and Severinos of the world at the moment.

Part 3: Featured Articles

The Baseball Is Juiced (Again)

Robert Arthur

This article originally appeared at Baseball Prospectus on April 5, 2019.

It started when the normally reliable Chris Sale got lit up for three homers by the Mariners in the Red Sox's season opener. It was part of a record number of taters that flew on Opening Day, as starters from Sale to Zack Greinke were taken deep by the handful. Then Christian Yelich hit a home run in each of his first four games, tying yet another MLB record, this one for consecutive games with a dinger to start a season.

It didn't take long for fans and players to begin whispering and tweeting about the baseballs being juiced again. It's early yet for us to come to any definitive conclusion about the 2019 season, but preliminary data shows that the baseball has returned to its aerodynamic peak. Whether that means this season will smash home run records like 2017 did remains to be seen.

Before home run explosion over the last few years, no one worried too much about the baseball's air resistance. While MLB and Rawlings (the company that manufactures the official baseballs) kept track of dozens of metrics to make sure that the ball was consistent from month to month, they didn't measure drag.

But drag is incredibly important in determining how likely a hitter is to knock one out of the park. As baseballs become more aerodynamic, they travel further given a certain initial velocity. A deep fly ball that might have been caught at the warning track can instead go into the first row of the stands. A three percent change in drag coefficient can work to add about five feet to a well-hit fly ball, which can in turn increase home runs league wide by an astounding 10-15 percent.

It's possible to measure the aerodynamics of the baseball using the pitch-tracking radars currently in place in each MLB ballpark. By calculating the loss of speed from when the pitch is released to when it crosses the plate, you can directly measure the drag coefficient on the baseball. I first wrote about the role of decreasing drag in boosting home runs in 2017, and MLB's commission of scientists and statisticians later confirmed that the more aerodynamic baseballs in use that year were largely to blame for the spike in home runs. The same commission rejected some alternate hypotheses, like rising temperatures and a league-wide boost in launch angle pushing more balls over the fence.

The current era has featured some large fluctuations in drag coefficient, leading to first an explosion in 2016 and 2017, and then a dialing back of homers last year. Curious about the record-breaking home run tallies in the last few days, I used the same methodology to measure the aerodynamics of the baseballs so far in 2019.

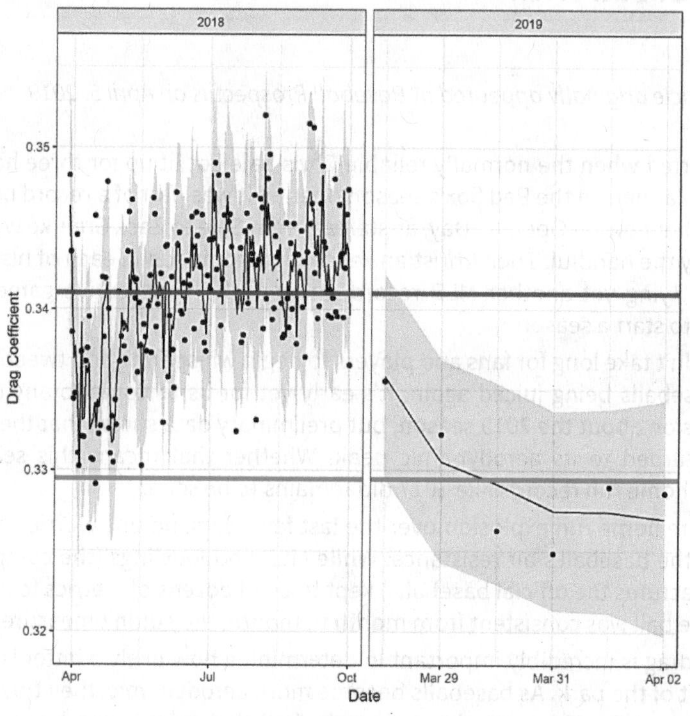

We're only a week into the 2019 season, but the drag numbers so far are among the lowest recorded in the last calendar year. With apologies for gory math, the current 2019 season average drag coefficient (the red line) would be below the 95 percent credible interval (the shaded area) for about nine-tenths of the 2018 season. (I used a Bayesian Random Walk model implemented in INLA to calculate these credible intervals, averaging the drag numbers in each game and adjusting for park.)

There were only a handful of six-day stretches in 2018 that had drag numbers below what we're seeing now, and most were in late June and early July. All of this means that 2019's data so far is quite a bit different than what we saw through most of last year.

These drag coefficients factor out the effects of temperature and air density, so they aren't a product of April cold. However, the numbers could be deceptive if the radars used to track pitches have changed from year to year. I consulted with some experts within baseball who were not aware of any specific modifications to the radar this year that could produce this pattern, but it's an important caveat of which to be aware.

On the one hand, it's only been six days, and we don't quite have the statistical basis to say that these drag coefficients are unprecedented compared to 2018. On the other hand, we've witnessed about 5,000 fastballs so far this season, so it's not as if our sample size is small. At least so far, the baseball has played like it's much more aerodynamic than it was last year. In fact, the current drag coefficient is really only comparable to 2017, when the baseballs were more aerodynamic than they had been in at least a decade.

It's not just fancy radar tracking indicating that the baseball is flying through the air more easily. The current number of home runs per game (as of this writing) is the highest it's been since the heady days of 2017, the year that teams and players broke dinger-related records everywhere you looked. That's especially remarkable considering that we're in what is typically the coldest part of the regular season, when lower temperatures and higher winds tend to suppress offense and keep balls in the air within the park. Comparing only from April to April, this year's rate of home runs per fly ball is even a little bit higher than it was in 2017.

With that said, the current measurements are no guarantee that 2019 will be another year of record-shattering homer hitting. The trouble with the drag measurements is that they are not consistent from June to August, from week to week, or even sometimes from day to day. Whether because of natural manufacturing variation or differences in the underlying supplies of cowhide and thread that go into the baseballs, drag has a tendency to fluctuate up and down over the course of a year. So the homers that fly in the first week of April wouldn't necessarily clear the fence a week later.

It's possible that this one-week drop in drag coefficient subsides and the baseball returns to its 2018 levels. On the other hand, it's almost equally probable that the ball becomes even more slippery and flies ever farther. Either way, it's clear that the baseball's air resistance is something to keep an eye on for the remainder of the 2019 season. ■

—Robert Arthur is an author of Baseball Prospectus.

The Moral Hazard of Playing It Safe

Craig Goldstein

This article originally appeared at Baseball Prospectus on August 6, 2019.

A couple days prior to the trade deadline, amidst a sea of tranquility posing as the lead up to the trade deadline, Bob Nightengale took to Twitter. Nightengale, who was probably wearing his pants backwards at the time, tweeted that MLB GMs were coming around on the idea that the unified trade deadline should be moved back from July 31 to August 15, so they could better assess their positions in the standings and whether they should buy or sell. To which I said:

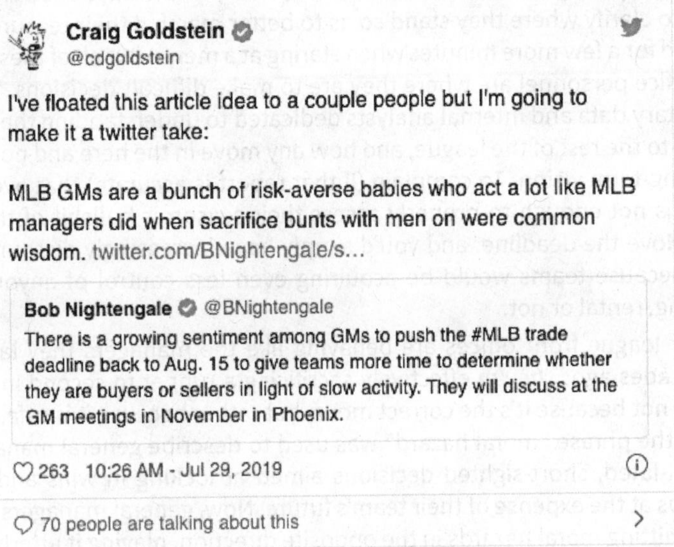

Craig Goldstein
@cdgoldstein
I've floated this article idea to a couple people but I'm going to make it a twitter take:
MLB GMs are a bunch of risk-averse babies who act a lot like MLB managers did when sacrifice bunts with men on were common wisdom. twitter.com/BNightengale/s...
Bob Nightengale @BNightengale
There is a growing sentiment among GMs to push the #MLB trade deadline back to Aug. 15 to give teams more time to determine whether they are buyers or sellers in light of slow activity. They will discuss at the GM meetings in November in Phoenix.
263 10:26 AM - Jul 29, 2019
70 people are talking about this

This might strike some as reductive and churlish. And it might be that, but it isn't really wrong, either. Jeff Quinton wrote a great piece discussing the environmental factors that enable front offices to avoid risk without upsetting the apple cart within their own fanbases. I don't believe that it goes far enough, however. His article gives us the proper framework through which to understand why these behaviors have been allowed to seep into front offices throughout the league. Understanding the reasons behind these actions are different from excusing them, though, and GMs should not be let off the hook for their non-competitive approach to the trade deadline (much less the offseason).

⚾ ⚾ ⚾

It's fair to say that fans as a group have rarely, if ever, been pro-player. It is also fair to say that in the time during and following the Moneyball revolution, the pendulum swung from fans who cared intensely about winning in the moment (and thus might be intolerant of a rebuilding approach) to fans who supported building a team that could compete throughout multiple seasons, viewing the playoffs as a crapshoot, with the thought that getting multiple bites at the apple was a better approach than taking a bigger bite in any one season.

There's nothing wrong with that approach, and I still find merit in that argument. However, it seems that the pendulum has swung too far in that direction. Teams are overvaluing some of the individual factors that make themselves long-term contenders rather than attempting to seize a championship when given the opportunity. It's a difficult needle to thread.

And surely, they (and those in similar positions) would have liked another two weeks to clarify where they stand so as to better marshal their resources. We've all asked for a few more minutes when staring at a menu. But all of these GMs and front office personnel are where they are to make difficult decisions. They have proprietary data and internal analysts dedicated to understanding their position relative to the rest of the league, and how any move in the here and now impacts their long-term vision. To complain (if that report is accurate) that over half the season is not enough to properly assess their season is bullshit of the highest order. Move the deadline, and you'd simply have increasingly discounted trade offers because teams would be acquiring even less control of anyone they're acquiring, rental or not.

Major league front offices are behaving like the managers they lampooned two decades ago. They're effectively sacrificing a runner to second in the ninth inning—not because it's the correct move, but rather because it is safe. It used to be that the phrase "moral hazard" was used to describe general managers who made ill-fated, short-sighted decisions aimed at locking in wins and securing their jobs at the expense of their team's future. Now, general managers are guilty of committing moral hazards in the opposite direction, playing it utterly safe and terrified of becoming scapegoats.

In lieu of bold action, they opt to pussyfoot around a current window of contention, choosing instead to play the long game and stack up years of control like they're blocks in a game of Jenga. GMs pass on signing quality players in free agency because the back-end of the deal might look bad, and because they might be able to squeeze out 70 percent of the production from a player who costs a tenth as much. That's a safer investment, too, because it's also hard to prove a negative—it's impossible to prove that Manny Machado would make the Mets a playoff team in 2019-2020, but it's easy to say that the back half of Robinson Cano's contract sucks. Owners, who rule over GM's jobs, are also humans with human brain processes that will always make the so-called albatross contract uglier than the road not taken.

These days, GMs are remembered for the bad deals they make and the surplus value they generate, not the acquisition of expensive, necessary talents that meet their market worth (or fall slightly short while still providing significant on-field value). And front offices know that one or two expensive misfires can cost them their jobs, no matter how many good deals they make.

No front office exemplifies this ethos more than the Toronto Blue Jays. General Manager Ross Atkins had this to say following the Blue Jays underwhelming trade deadline:

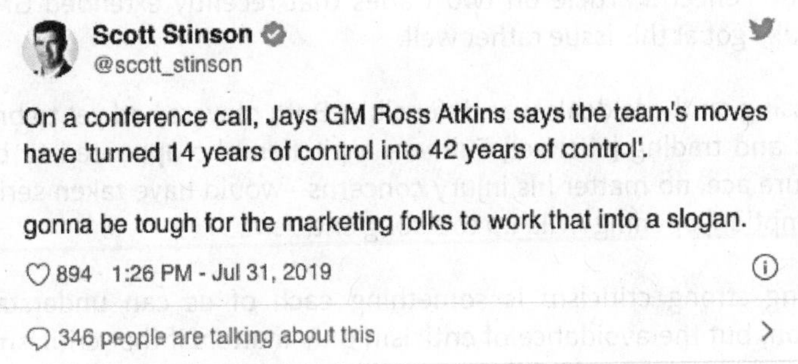
Scott Stinson
@scott_stinson

On a conference call, Jays GM Ross Atkins says the team's moves have 'turned 14 years of control into 42 years of control'.

gonna be tough for the marketing folks to work that into a slogan.

894 1:26 PM - Jul 31, 2019

346 people are talking about this

This is by no means the first time that an executive will cite years of control to justify their actions, which is often just another way of saying "don't look at what we got, look at how much we got of it." Atkins touts quantity to elide the discussion of quality—either, that of the players acquired, or those given up. Remember: the other teams presumably value years of control, too.

Atkins also had some thoughts to offer regarding free agents back in early 2018:

Pitch Talks
@PitchTalks
#BlueJays GM Ross Atkins "when you're talking about free agency you're talking about aging players and the trend of overpaying a player's aging curves has come to an end across baseball"
♡ 62 6:09 PM - Feb 1, 2018 · The Rivoli
59 people are talking about this

This ignores, of course, whether the player can create enough value in the front end of a contract to justify the longer term of a deal, and the decline that often occurs in the back end. It also ignores whether the player can fill a need the team requires and put them in a position to compete for and win a championship. But as teams seemingly avoid contention at all, where they might end up having to consider and later justify some of these tough decisions, we still see risk-averse approaches.

Anthony Fenech's article on two trades that recently extended GM Al Avila didn't make got at this issue rather well:

> Passing on those deals was defensible: Both players had yet to break out and trading [Michael] Fulmer—a pitcher who appeared to be a future ace, no matter his injury concerns—would have taken serious gumption, opening Avila up to strong criticism.

Avoiding strong criticism is something each of us can understand as a motivation, but the avoidance of criticism only matters if that criticism is valid. In Fulmer's case, shoving his injury concerns aside affects not only the years that the team controls him (he is currently missing a full season due to Tommy John surgery) but also the quality of those seasons, as his knee and elbow injuries combined to dampen his effectiveness even when healthy enough to pitch. But it was easy to present the then-current image of Fulmer as a top of the rotation pitcher who the team had under its domain for the next five seasons as something to build around. The status quo isn't nearly as often second-guessed as a decision that disrupts it.

⚾ ⚾ ⚾

MLB GMs are risk-averse to a fault. They are ivy-educated and consulting firm-approved, and yet they can't seem to avoid leaving wins on the table in their all-consuming lust for a non-existent $/WAR championship. They are supposed to zig when everyone else zags, and not merely pay lip service to the idea of zigging through a calculated PR plan built on convincing the fan base their approach is novel when it actually apes most of their competitors. Instead they've become far more concerned with making safe, accepted-by-the-new-common-wisdom decisions, such that our prior understanding of what a moral hazard is has become inverted.

I can't blame them entirely, and not only because of the reasons that Quinton illuminated in his article, but also because of the damage wrought by the introduction of the second wild card (WC2) spot. MLB's desire to have more teams in playoff contention has sparked anti-competitive behavior. Teams know now that they do not need to swing big as they assemble their roster because there is a good chance that a mediocre team can either catch fire and capture a division, or muddle along until they back into the WC2.

Simultaneously, the one-game playoff has neutered the WC1, putting an entire season on the flip of a coin like some sort of baseball-obsessed Anton Chigurh. While the one-game playoff makes sense as a way to increase the value of winning a division, it also means that if a front office doesn't like its chances of overcoming a behemoth like the Dodgers or Astros in the offseason, they have few incentives to chase glory. Similarly, the relative inaction in the NL Central at the trade deadline—despite a wide open division—can be explained by the idea that any high-variance investment could still result in only a wild card (or worse) result, given the mere two months left in the season to make an impact.

As stated at the top, we should not confuse reasons for excuses. The implementation of the second wild card is just one of many environmental factors that influence how each front office operates. I am convinced that it is one of the larger factors, but I am also convinced that organizations need to shed the yoke of "efficiency at all costs" so that they can instead pursue competition, as the spirit of the game intends. Until they do, we're all deadline losers.

—Craig Goldstein is an author of Baseball Prospectus.

Index of Names

Abreu, Albert 94, 99
Alcantara, Kevin 92, 104
Andújar, Miguel 85
Avilán, Luis 51
Barrett, Jake 94
Bettis, Chad 53
Britton, Zack 55
Cabello, Antonio 106
Cessa, Luis 57
Chapman, Aroldis 59
Cole, Gerrit 61
Contreras, Roansy 94, 104
Dominguez, Jasson 86, 98
Duran, Ezequiel 92, 103
Estrada, Thairo 20
Florial, Estevan 87, 102
Ford, Mike 22
Frazier, Clint 24
Garcia, Deivi 90, 97
Gardner, Brett 26
Germán, Domingo 63
German, Frank 94, 106
Gil, Luis 94, 100
Gomez, Yoendrys 94, 105
Gore, Terrance 92
Granite, Zack 92
Green, Chad 65
Hale, David 67
Happ, J.A. 69
Heller, Ben 94
Herrera, Rosell 92
Hicks, Aaron 28
Higashioka, Kyle 30
Holder, Jonathan 71
Judge, Aaron 32
Kahnle, Tommy 73
King, Mike 94, 105
Kratz, Erik 92
Kriske, Brooks 94
Lail, Brady 94
LeMahieu, DJ 34
Loaisiga, Jonathan 94
Lyons, Tyler 94
Medina, Luis 94, 99
Montgomery, Jordan 91
Morales, Kendrys 92
Munoz, Anderson 109
Nelson, Nick 94, 108
Ottavino, Adam 75
Paxton, James 77
Pereira, Everson 92
Sabathia, CC 79
Sánchez, Gary 38
Schmidt, Clarke 94, 103
Seigler, Anthony 92, 107
Severino, Luis 81
Sikkema, T.J. 92, 106
Smith, Canaan 92
Smith, Josh 92, 108
Stanton, Giancarlo 36
Stowers, Josh 107
Tanaka, Masahiro 83

New York Yankees 2020

Tarpley, Stephen 94
Tauchman, Mike 40
Torres, Gleyber 43
Tropeano, Nick 94
Tulowitzki, Troy 88
Urshela, Gio 45
Vizcaino, Alexander 108
Voit, Luke 47
Volpe, Anthony 89, 101
Wade, Tyler 49
Yajure, Miguel 94